Using Formative Assessment in the RTI Framework

Kay Burke
Eileen Depka

Solution Tree | Press
a division of

Solution Tree

555 North Morton Street
Bloomington, IN 47404
800.733.6786 (toll free) / 812.336.7700
FAX: 812.336.7790

email: info@solution-tree.com
solution-tree.com

Printed in the United States of America
15 14 13 12 11   1 2 3 4 5

FSC
Mixed Sources
Product group from well-managed
forests and other controlled sources

Cert no. SW-COC-002283
www.fsc.org
© 1996 Forest Stewardship Council

Library of Congress Cataloging-in-Publication Data

Burke, Kay.
  Using formative assessment in the RTI framework / Kay Burke, Eileen Depka.
      p. cm.
  Includes bibliographical references and index.
  ISBN 978-1-935249-74-0 (perfect bound) -- ISBN 978-1-935249-75-7 (library edition)
  1. Educational tests and measurements. 2. Learning disabled children--Rating of. 3. Response to intervention
(Learning disabled children) I. Depka, Eileen. II. Title.
  LB3051.B7952 2011
  371.260973--dc22
                                    2011008095

Solution Tree
Jeffrey C. Jones, CEO & President

Solution Tree Press
President: Douglas M. Rife
Publisher: Robert D. Clouse
Vice President of Production: Gretchen Knapp
Managing Production Editor: Caroline Wise
Senior Production Editor: Lesley Bolton
Copy Editor: Rachel Rosolina
Proofreader: Elisabeth Abrams
Text Designer: Raven Bongiani
Cover Designer: Orlando Angel

This book is dedicated to all teachers and administrators who are committed every day to the task of helping students meet and exceed standards while developing a lifelong love of learning.

Acknowledgments

It may take a village to make a difference in the lives of students, but it takes Solution Tree to make a difference in the lives of authors. It all starts at the top, and Jeff Jones is a force of nature whose vision for education inspires us all. Douglas Rife, Robb Clouse, and Gretchen Knapp, the leadership team at Solution Tree Press, provide a level of organization, integrity, and excellence unsurpassed in educational publishing. Their editorial and graphic design team members excel. We would like to thank Lesley Bolton for her insightful and thoughtful editing and Caroline Wise for her creative and humorous management style. Writing a book is never easy, but the process has been so much more enjoyable working with a team of true professionals and really nice people. Of course, the book is just the beginning. Claudia Wheatley, the best author liaison ever, and Terri Martin, Shannon Ritz, and the professional development team support the ongoing relationship through conferences and workshops. It is a privilege to play a small role in the most dynamic company in education.

We would like to give a special thanks to the following educators, who have contributed their work to the book.

Carrollton City Middle School, Carrollton City Schools, Carrollton, Georgia:
Dr. Kent Edwards, superintendent; Erin McGinnis, director of school improvement and curriculum/instruction; Trent North, principal of Carrollton Middle School; Debra B. Williams, retired administrator; and teachers Sheri Davis and Pamela Russell Smith

Sharp Creek Elementary School, Carroll County Schools, Carrollton, Georgia:
Deaidra Wilson, principal; and teachers Donna Barnett, Tara Ferguson, James Kirk, Sandra Prince, Jennifer Vaught, Lisa Weaver, and Keya Yarbrough

DeKalb County Schools, Decatur, Georgia:
Yvonne Stroud, teacher at Champion Middle School

Professional Association of Georgia Educators (PAGE), Atlanta, Georgia:
Ann H. Stucke, PhD, director, Teacher Academy and Professional Learning Institutes; Nadeen Pagano, administrative assistant; and teachers Jacquelyn Maddox Brownlee (Tift County), Shiona Shanel Drummer (Bibb County), Cody K. Flowers (Chatham County), Christina Gilbert (Chatham County), Carla Hamilton (Muscogee County), Jennifer Kanzler (Marietta City Schools), Jessica Ellen Ruark (McDuffie County), Lindsey Sherrouse (Warren County), and Jamie Strickland (Cherokee County)

Solution Tree Press would like to thank the following reviewers:

Betty Eisenberg
District RTI Coordinator
Orange County Public Schools
Orlando, Florida

Sharon Frys
Assistant Superintendent, Instructional and Student Services
Community Consolidated School District 93
Bloomingdale, Illinois

Diane Hart
K–12 Learning Systems and Programs Manager
Cobb County School District
Marietta, Georgia

Linda Kaminski
Assistant Superintendent, Educational Services
Upland Unified School District
Upland, California

Bradley Niebling
Alignment Specialist
Heartland Area Education Agency 11
Johnston, Iowa

Lynne Spiller
Director of Research and Evaluation
Creighton School District
Phoenix, Arizona

Table of Contents

About the Authors

Since 1992, **KAY BURKE** has facilitated professional development workshops for teachers and administrators, delivered keynote addresses, and presented at conferences sponsored by the Association for Supervision and Curriculum Development, Learning Forward (formerly the National Staff Development Council), the National Association of Elementary School Principals, the National Association of Secondary School Principals, the National Middle School Association, the International Reading Association, and Solution Tree, as well as international conferences throughout Australia and Canada.

Kay has written and edited books in the areas of standards-based learning, performance assessment, classroom management, mentoring, and portfolios. Some of her best-selling books include *How to Assess Authentic Learning*, fifth edition (2009); *What to Do With the Kid Who . . . : Developing Cooperation, Self-Discipline, and Responsibility in the Classroom*, third edition (2008); and *The Portfolio Connection: Student Work Linked to Standards*, third edition (2008). Her book *From Standards to Rubrics in Six Steps: Tools for Assessing Student Learning* was named a 2007 finalist for the Distinguished Achievement Award from the Association of Educational Publishers and is in its third edition (2011). She is also the author of *Balanced Assessment: From Formative to Summative*.

Kay received a bachelor of arts degree from Florida Atlantic University, a master's degree from University of Central Florida, a specialist degree from Emory University, and a doctorate from Georgia State University in Atlanta. Her dissertation focused on helping students improve their performance on standardized tests.

EILEEN DEPKA is the assistant superintendent of educational services, which includes curriculum, instruction, assessment, special education, and educational technology, in the School District of Elmbrook, Wisconsin. Some aspects of her role include working with continuous improvement planning, data analysis, and response to intervention. Eileen has worked as a content adviser on educational videos and written online courses. As an instructor at the graduate level, she has taught courses in assessment, curriculum design, and grading and reporting practices.

Eileen presents at the local, regional, and national levels on such topics as assessment, data collection and analysis, continuous school improvement, best practices, and differentiation, and facilitates workshops on a variety of topics with schools and districts. She is the author of *Designing Rubrics for Mathematics*, *Designing Assessment for Mathematics*, and *The Data Guidebook for Teachers and Leaders: Tools for Continuous Improvement*, and is a contributing author to *Data Enhanced Leadership*.

Eileen received a bachelor's degree from the University of Wisconsin-Milwaukee and a master's degree from Cardinal Stritch University. She is currently in the doctoral leadership program at Cardinal Stritch University.

To book Kay Burke or Eileen Depka for professional development, contact pd@solution-tree .com.

Introduction

According to the National Center for Education Statistics (Snyder, 2010), 2,983,000 students were expected to graduate from public high school in 2009–2010. However, approximately 8 percent (over 250,000) of those students dropped out of school. Although the dropout rate may not be solely the result of needs not being met, it is likely that if students had experienced a greater level of success in school, many more would have graduated.

Response to intervention (RTI), a framework for meeting the needs of students, and formative assessment, a process for evaluating student understanding and using data to make instructional decisions, have the potential to positively impact this issue. When formative assessment is coupled with RTI, teachers can catch students before they fall too far behind. Formative assessment is not only an important component of effective instruction within the RTI framework; it is a key feature of instructional design (Brown-Chidsey & Steege, 2005). Linking the results of formative assessment to instructional change can enhance learning (Griffiths, Parson, Burns, VanDerHeyden, & Tilly, 2007). Adjusting instruction, varying classroom strategies, altering assessment measures, and increasing the use of data influence student success in school.

RTI and formative assessment fit naturally together. In fact, high-quality instruction and formative assessments lay a solid foundation for an effective RTI structure: teachers observe students, collect data using formative assessment tools, and make instructional decisions related to their students' ongoing needs (Mellard & Johnson, 2008). Monitoring student progress and adjusting instruction are routine to the formative assessment process, both resulting in strengthening the foundation of the RTI framework.

This book is intended for teachers and administrators who want to better understand the basics of RTI and its connection to formative assessment. Our goal is to provide educators with ample information and ideas that will help them base their instructional decisions on the results of effective formative assessment practices. Whether experienced or inexperienced in the use of formative assessment and data collection and analysis, readers will find useful tips and strategies that will advance their knowledge and understanding toward the goal of increasing student achievement.

Part 1 establishes a basic understanding of formative assessment and RTI. Part 2 provides tools and tips for various methods of administering formative assessments and gathering the resulting data. Teachers can use assessment results to improve the caliber of instructional decision making (Popham, 2002). Therefore, we designed tools to assist teachers in accurately assessing student performance. As a whole, this book provides information, examples, and devices to assess student needs and evaluate progress and achievement within an RTI framework.

Chapter 1 provides an overview of the background, structure, and components of RTI. Assessment is a crucial component within the RTI framework, and formative assessment, in particular, plays an important role. Chapter 2 describes formative assessment in greater detail, focusing on how teachers can use formative assessment to differentiate and improve their instruction to meet the needs of their students. Data analysis is also essential to the RTI process. Therefore, chapter 3 suggests a four-step, systematic approach to data collection and analysis and provides a variety of data collection and display methods and questions to inspire thought and action based on data. Chapter 4 combines RTI, formative assessment, and data analysis to create an ideal system for increasing student achievement.

The remaining chapters highlight and detail the tools that will help teachers make the most of formative assessment within an RTI framework. Chapter 5 defines feedback and reflection in relation to RTI and provides examples of related tools. The purpose of both feedback and reflection is to help students and teachers better understand current performance, compare it to the desired level of performance, and take action to close any gap between the two. Chapter 6 shows how checklists can act as a form of scaffolding to help students organize a project or performance and complete each step of the process. Checklists can also help students self-assess their social skills and behavior patterns so they become more aware of how their actions affect their academic achievement. Chapter 7 highlights different types of rubrics and includes steps that lead to creating quality rubrics. Chapter 8 explores performance tasks, which present problem scenarios that are relevant to students' lives. Performance tasks use the structure of project-based or problem-based learning to promote 21st century skills, such as organizing and analyzing information, solving problems, conducting experiments, integrating technology, and collaborating with others.

The pages that follow explore the components of quality formative assessment and data analysis. *Using Formative Assessment in the RTI Framework* provides teachers and administrators with information, tools, and techniques that they can use to adjust instruction and increase levels of student understanding and achievement.

Part 1

Understanding RTI and Formative Assessment

Chapter 1
Overview of RTI

RTI is a structure that aligns instruction and systems of assessment, data collection and analysis, and interventions to best meet the academic and behavioral needs of students. It is based on the belief that all students—including English learners, students with disabilities, students who are economically disadvantaged, and students of all ethnic backgrounds—can learn if they are given the proper materials, strategies, and interventions. The goal of RTI is to maximize student achievement through the use of effective instruction strategies while teaching and promoting behaviors that are supportive of the learning environment. Think of RTI as the framework for a service-delivery system that includes high-quality instruction, evidence-based academic and behavioral interventions, frequent monitoring of student progress, the regular and consistent use of data for decision making, and team collaboration. Evidence-based interventions are implemented to increase the probability of a successful outcome (Brown-Chidsey & Steege, 2005). The intensity and frequency of interventions are adjusted according to student responses throughout the implementation.

Although RTI is considered a general education initiative, its foundation is rooted in special education law; the term was incorporated into the 2004 Individuals with Disabilities Education Act (IDEA, http://idea.ed.gov). Educators recognized problems in the deficit model of special education and called for reform. The old model was problematic in that students were not identified as having special educational needs until a large deficit was apparent. In this "wait to fail" model, students could not qualify for special education until they experienced a level in their academic performance that was years below that of their peers. As a result, students did not receive special education services until the discrepancy was such that closing the gap was difficult and often unlikely.

The RTI model is built on the premise that a structure of appropriate curricula, instruction, assessments, and interventions, all based on scientific research, provides a framework in which students will have the best chance at academic and behavioral success. When a student is recognized as having a need that requires a specific intervention, the need is addressed, progress is monitored, and adjustments are made as necessary. Should the student not respond, a different or more intensive intervention is employed. A two-year deficit is not required before action is taken. If students continue to struggle and evidence indicates the need, the potential result is a special education referral. Special education referral and identification are not the main focus of RTI but can be the outcomes for those students who don't respond to the repeated use of interventions matched to their specific needs. Evidence and the constant and consistent use of data are foundational components of the RTI process.

As the U.S. Department of Education does not endorse any one structure for RTI, states can create their own to best suit their needs. However, according to the U.S. Department of Education, states must incorporate certain components into the model, such as a strong research base and frequent monitoring of student progress.

RTI Structure

The RTI structure is often illustrated as a three-tier pyramid with Tier 1 at the bottom and Tier 3 at the top. A four-tier approach is another option. The fourth tier indicates the referral process used to evaluate students for a potential special education need. The focus herein will be on the three-tier model as it is the most common.

Tier 1

The components that make up Tier 1 create a solid foundation for RTI. The basis of Tier 1 is a high-quality, guaranteed, and viable curriculum including standards-based instruction supported by research-based materials.

The regular education classroom is the setting for Tier 1. Within Tier 1, teachers commit to devoting time to each subject and curricular fidelity. The time commitment typically includes a minimum of ninety minutes of reading and sixty minutes of mathematics per day at the elementary level, and appropriate time is allotted to content, concepts, and application of understanding. The strong emphasis on reading and math is due to federal legislation regarding state testing and accountability in those two areas. Mandated state testing takes place in grades 3 through 8 and again in high school (Mellard & Johnson, 2008).

An expectation of Tier 1 is the use of instructional strategies that have proven to be effective. RTI encourages teachers to vary instruction to create a constant atmosphere of learning (Fisher & Frey, 2010). Therefore, strategies should include flexible grouping, small-group instruction and support, and differentiated instructional techniques.

Another key component of Tier 1 is universal screening, which generates data tied to standards. The data are used to compare students to their grade-level peers to measure individual student success. All students participate in the same assessment, typically three times per year, to measure growth and to identify those who are experiencing challenges. In advance of the assessment, a school or district team identifies scores that indicate a student is struggling and may need an additional intervention, a change in teaching strategy, small-group support, or differentiation. Anyone performing below this point should be monitored.

Formative assessment, another essential component, supports students at all RTI tiers. Formative assessment is the process of using quality assessments to measure student understanding, collecting data to record student progress, and making instructional decisions based on the data. At Tier 1, formative assessment data are used to guide instruction to meet the needs of various students. Multiple types of assessments are needed to create a complete picture of student understanding, and the teacher must keep records of student progress.

Students who do not make acceptable progress in Tier 1 are provided with Tier 2 support. This occurs only after it is clear that instructional and curricular fidelity are evident, appropriate amounts of time have been devoted to the subject area, classroom interventions have been unsuccessful, and attempts have been made to respond to the needs of the students, but methods, although appropriately implemented, did not result in acceptable student growth.

Tier 2

Tier 2 interventions are small-group interventions that take place for a minimum of thirty minutes, three days per week. It is important that specific interventions be implemented as intended to achieve the highest levels of success. Students receiving these interventions have demonstrated a significantly different level of classroom performance when compared to others at their grade level within Tier 1. The cut scores earned by these students on previous assessments indicated that there was a need to watch student growth and continued progress. Placing these students in a Tier 2 intervention was a reaction to an identified need after monitoring classroom performance and progress at Tier 1.

Tier 2 implementation often requires the flexible use of personnel and creative scheduling. These interventions are completed in addition to the regular classroom instruction, so the intervention for a specific content area needs to occur at a different time than the regularly scheduled instruction for that content area. The teacher must provide a consistent time frame for the intervention. Tier 2 interventions do not replace classroom instruction; they are used to address the deficits identified during Tier 1 by targeting instruction to meet the needs of students identified through the analysis of assessment data.

Tier 2 interventions can take place in the general education classroom, administered by the general education teacher. Alternatively, intervention specialists, qualified personnel, or content-area specialists can take charge of Tier 2 interventions, depending on available staff, time, and expertise. Because Tier 2 interventions are in addition to the regular classroom instruction experienced in Tier 1, the interventions often take place outside of the classroom. A location is identified by the interventionist. This could be a regular education classroom, a resource room, a media center, a library, or any available space that meets the needs of the group.

Monitoring progress is an important aspect of Tier 2. Teachers identify and use progress-monitoring assessments to clearly measure the skills associated with the intervention, and they administer the assessments on a regular, more frequent basis, typically at least bimonthly. The teachers usually chart and share the assessment results with the students so that they can see their growth and the tangible results of their participation in the intervention.

When students experience success at Tier 2, they no longer need Tier 2 interventions but will continue to receive the levels of support provided in Tier 1. Students who do not experience success may receive different interventions, or the intensity of the intervention may be increased. Following such adjustments, if students still don't experience success, a Tier 3 intervention may be necessary.

Tier 3

A Tier 3 intervention is intensive and usually individualized. Students who fail to show adequate progress in Tier 2 interventions are provided with a Tier 3 intervention plan tailored to best meet their individual needs. Interventions take place daily for an hour or a class period, in addition to regular classroom instruction. Intervention specialists, qualified personnel, or content-area specialists usually implement the interventions and complete the progress monitoring. Interventions take place in a space identified by the interventionist.

Tier 3 interventions occur as long as needed, assuming that progress continues to be made. Progress monitoring, a crucial element of Tier 3 interventions, is used to determine the student's response to the intervention. Progress-monitoring results are charted and shared with the student.

Students who receive appropriate instruction and interventions are likely to make adequate progress unless they have a more specific need. If a student does not make adequate progress at Tier 3, data will be generated from multiple forms of assessment including universal screening and progress monitoring, providing a variety of information about the student and his or her response to instruction and intervention. When acceptable progress is not being made, a referral for evaluation for special education may result following a data review, typically conducted by a student support team or intervention team. This team analyzes the data and decides whether extended time with an intervention is needed or if a disability might be hindering student growth.

Figure 1.1 examines what is accomplished at each tier and when, where, and by whom the interventions of each tier are implemented.

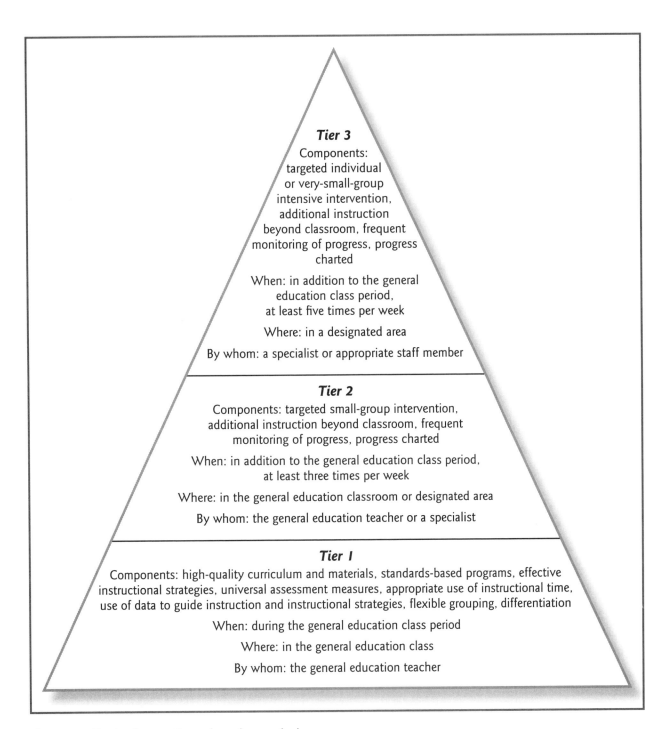

Figure 1.1: Tier implementation: who, when, and where.

Intervention Teams

Intervention teams ensure the consistent and systematic implementation of RTI practices. Sometimes called the RTI team, the intervention team manages the decision-making process regarding student progress, data, and interventions. This team also makes appropriate decisions on instructional programming (Bender & Shores, 2007).

A team typically includes the school principal, a psychologist, teachers, and others who have contact with the student. When a student is not experiencing acceptable progress, his or her teacher requests an intervention team meeting. The team analyzes the current situation, discusses which tier is appropriate, determines next steps, and identifies interventions needed for success. In addition, they discuss fidelity to determine whether the student's response to previous interventions was unsuccessful because the intervention didn't meet the student's needs or because the implementation was questionable.

The intervention team determines who will implement interventions as well as when and where implementation will occur. The team may set the tentative length of time needed to determine the probability of student success and schedule a follow-up meeting to continue monitoring the situation. Effective teams focus on answering four basic questions:

1. What is the current situation with the student?

2. What is the potential cause of the situation?

3. What response is required to ensure academic or behavioral growth?

4. Did the response work, and what next steps are required?

Jim Wright (2007) of Intervention Central suggests that teams develop an intervention bank. Teams discuss common teacher concerns and identify research-based interventions. Over time, interventions are categorized and organized so that they are accessible and consistent across the grade level and school. Although some interventions may be grade specific, others might be available at multiple levels. With the identification and use of consistent interventions, training and funds can be dedicated to the interventions deemed most successful.

Figure 1.2 illustrates the expected percent of student success at each RTI tier. Crucial to success is fidelity to curriculum, instruction, assessment, and intervention at each tier. School intervention teams should monitor the percent of total student success to determine the level of schoolwide success of curricula, instruction, assessments, and interventions at each tier. This function can also be accomplished by a school improvement team, whose responsibility is to monitor school goals and measure academic and behavioral growth throughout the school.

If, for example, 35 percent of students are in need of Tier 2 interventions, it is likely that there is a fidelity issue at Tier 1. Instead of assuming the students are the problem, the team should discuss whether a better match could have been made between the students and classroom strategies. Was the appropriate amount of time spent on instruction? Was formative assessment used to adjust instruction to meet student needs? Could other factors be interfering with student progress? Keep in mind this rule of thumb: "if 80% of students are not performing at or above proficiency levels, then universal core instruction is not working adequately" (Howell, Patton, & Deiotte, 2008, p. 106). If students are not successful, the deficit may be attributed to the classroom instructional approaches not effectively meeting student needs rather than the students themselves. Such a situation requires strategy adjustments so that the greatest number of students can experience success at Tier 1.

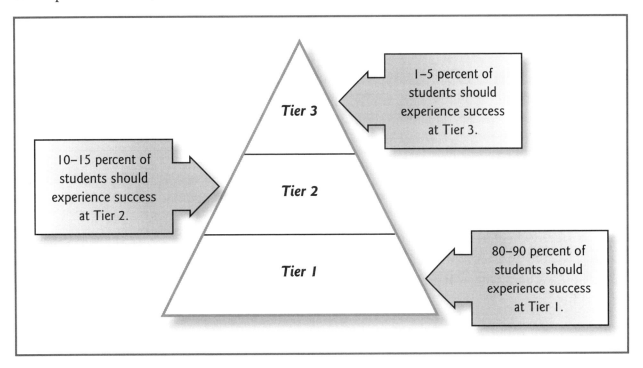

Figure 1.2: Expected rate of academic and behavioral success.

RTI and Assessment

Four types of assessment are necessary for the effective implementation of RTI: (1) universal screening, (2) progress-monitoring assessments, (3) diagnostic testing, and (4) formative assessments.

Universal screening refers to exactly what its name indicates. It includes assessment measures identified in specific content areas that are administered to all students at specified grade levels. Schools typically schedule universal screenings three times each year. Teachers collect baseline data in the fall, and growth is measured midyear and in the spring. Scores reflecting an expected level of achievement are preidentified by the school intervention team or district RTI team. Those scores are used to compare a student's progress to that of his or her peers. Deficits are identified and appropriate responses are determined and implemented. Although this is usually done by the classroom teacher, some districts have assessment coordinators or resource teachers who help with these efforts.

Progress-monitoring assessments are necessary for students participating in Tier 2 and Tier 3 interventions. These assessments are easy to administer and usually take no more than a few minutes. Teachers conduct progress-monitoring assessments frequently—at least bimonthly, but most often weekly. Author John Hoover (2009), a former special educator, calls progress monitoring the systematic gathering of data to provide evidence that the student is responding appropriately to the strategy or intervention. Through frequent monitoring, student progress—or lack of progress—can be closely tracked. Data from each of the progress-monitoring assessments are graphed and analyzed. If expected growth is not attained during an acceptable length of time, another intervention will need to be identified. The newly identified intervention might be another Tier 2 intervention or, if warranted, a Tier 3 intervention. Data analysis includes an evaluation of intervention implementation to determine whether the intervention was implemented as intended with the appropriate frequency and consistency. This is necessary to ensure that student assessment results are due to the student's response to the intervention and not an issue of intervention fidelity.

The intervention team may recommend a form of *diagnostic testing* when a student is not responding to Tier 3 interventions. These diagnostic tests are designed to identify areas of weakness in the learning process and are typically administered by trained individuals. Diagnostic tests are used to help identify the complexity and origin of a student's deficit. These assessments identify reasons that a student is experiencing learning difficulties and may indicate that special education services are required. Such tests would likely include ability measures and tests of basic skills.

Formative assessments are necessary to effectively implement RTI. While progress-monitoring assessments are used to measure the effectiveness of a specific intervention, formative assessments are used on a regular basis to determine the progress being made in the classroom and to adjust instruction or instructional strategies in response to the assessment results. By analyzing the data gathered from these assessments, teachers are able to make instructional decisions, which can improve the effectiveness of the instruction and increase student performance and understanding. Individual student progress can also be compared to the progress of others in the classroom. Over time, these assessments can provide information about whether progress is adequate or if a specific intervention is required. Formative assessments can include teacher-made tests, logs, journals, checklists, rubrics, reflections, exit slips, and other tools that provide valuable information regarding student understanding. Without formative assessments, teachers would be proceeding blindly and guessing at which strategies and techniques are most effective. According to Austin Buffum, Mike Mattos, and Chris Weber (2009), authors of *Pyramid Response to Intervention*:

> Without timely assessment information, a school's intervention program assumes a "buckshot" approach, with teachers randomly "firing" broad intervention efforts and hoping that they "hit" a few students. Frequent, formative common assessments also provide the foundation for the progress monitoring needed to properly implement response to intervention. (p. 52)

Formative assessments will be explored in further detail in the next chapter. Although all types of assessment used in the RTI framework have an important role to play, the focus on formative assessment in this book is due to its specific benefits within the RTI structure and the process it promotes. Formative assessments are designed to measure student understanding.

Teachers administer the assessment, collect and interpret the data, and immediately respond with a change in content, method, or strategy. This process addresses student needs as they are recognized, without delay or the formality of consulting with an intervention team. The formative assessment process has the potential of having the greatest impact on the student success rate at Tier 1 because it is closest to the classroom teacher, it is the most frequent method of assessment, and it can have an immediate response or action.

In Conclusion

RTI is a tiered framework designed to identify system responses to student academic and behavioral needs. Key components include evidence-based curricula and interventions, systems of assessment and data analysis, and collaborative efforts that concentrate on meeting the needs of struggling students. RTI is based on the belief that all students are capable of achieving high levels of success if their needs are matched to materials, strategies, and interventions. The successful implementation of RTI requires collaboration and professional development, and schools need to adequately embed systems of assessment and data analysis in the process.

When it is well-implemented, RTI works for almost all struggling students. Subgroups are able to experience high academic gains, and even the most challenging students can be positively impacted (Bender, 2009).

Chapter 2
Overview of Formative Assessment

No chapter on assessment would be complete without a pretest to determine prior knowledge, so let's start with a quick question.

A process by which educators use student responses to specially created or naturally occurring stimuli in order to make inferences about student knowledge, skill, or affective status is:

A. Educational assessment

B. Educational testing

C. Educational measurement

D. A & B

E. All of the above

If you answered "E" (all of the above), you are correct. According to assessment expert W. James Popham (2006), "the words *assessment*, *measurement*, and *testing* are fundamentally synonymous" (p. 5). However, educators prefer to use the term *assessment* because it "creates a more comprehensive and more palatable image than either *measurement* or *testing*" (p. 4).

The word *assess* comes from the Latin *assidere*, which means "to sit beside and guide." In education, assessment is the process of gathering evidence about student learning to improve student learning. Assessment plays a critical role in the instructional process and has multiple instructional purposes.

In addition to being used to identify why a student is experiencing learning difficulties, *diagnostic assessments* can also be administered at the beginning of a learning segment to determine students' prior knowledge and skills. Such an assessment could be a formal standardized test, a district benchmark test, or a teacher-made pretest. It helps the teacher determine where students are in relation to learning goals.

Formative assessments occur throughout the learning segment and can be more informal because they are not usually graded. Quizzes, rehearsals, conversations, observations, rough drafts—these ongoing assessments provide specific feedback to teachers for the purpose of guiding teaching to improve learning (Wiggins & McTighe, 2007). Formative assessments also provide specific feedback to the students for the purpose of improving the quality of their products or performances, clarifying their thinking, and promoting a deeper understanding of important ideas and concepts.

At the end of each learning segment, the teacher has to make a judgment about whether or not a student has met the learning goal. *Summative assessments* are used to determine the degree to which the student has met the goal. The results of the summative assessments are factored into the summative evaluation—or grade—given at the end of the marking period.

Educators use multiple sources of assessment information to evaluate individual students. Author Peter W. Airasian (2000) states, "Evaluation occurs after assessment information has been collected, synthesized, and thought about, because that is when the teacher is in a position to make informed judgments" (p. 10). Teachers use this interpretation of the data to make an inference about the student's ability to meet learning goals. This inference takes many forms depending on the situation, but it usually is symbolized by a letter grade, a percentage grade, or a label such as "meets expectations" or "exceeds standards." The evaluation completes the formal learning cycle.

Figure 2.1 provides an overview of the purposes of assessment.

The Importance of Formative Assessments

Instead of using assessments only as evaluation tools to mark the end of a learning segment or instructional unit, "more and more teachers today realize that formative assessments offer exactly what they have always wanted: a practical and efficient means to make their teaching better and to help all their students learn better" (Guskey, 2009, p. 1). When formative assessments are used on an ongoing basis, teachers can see almost immediately what is working and what is not working. For example, if students are asked to write a thesis statement for an informational writing piece, teachers can review these statements and quickly determine quality. If many students have problems with the assignment, the teacher could decide to reteach the lesson by using more examples of effective thesis statements and writing a few statements with the whole class. The teacher could also provide a short criteria checklist, such as the one shown in figure 2.2, that includes guiding questions to help students through the process.

Diagnostic Assessment

Purpose: To determine students' ability in relation to learning goals

Timing: The beginning of the learning segment (pretests, needs assessments, universal screening)

Formative Assessments

Purpose: To provide ongoing feedback to teachers about the effectiveness of their instruction meeting the diverse needs of their students and to students about their progress (or lack of progress) in meeting or exceeding learning goals

Timing: Throughout the learning segment

Summative Assessments

Purpose: To measure student achievement related to learning goals

Timing: The end of the learning segment

Evaluation

Purpose: To make an inference about the student's ability to meet learning goals using all assessment data

Timing: The end of the grading period (quarter, semester, year)

Figure 2.1: Purposes of assessment.

Thesis Statement

Did you state the main idea of your paper?
What was it? _____

Did you write one controlling idea that you will develop in paragraph one of the body of your paper?
What was it? _____

Did you write a second controlling idea that you will develop in paragraph two of the body of your paper?
What was it? _____

Did you write a third controlling idea that you consider to be the strongest argument and will develop in paragraph three of the body of your paper to prove your thesis statement?
What was it? _____

Figure 2.2: Checklist for writing thesis statements.

Teachers can use the checklist with the whole class, a group of students who are experiencing problems, or individual students who need more practice. The checklist is just one example of a formative assessment tool that provides immediate feedback targeted to the goals of both the teachers and the students. Formative assessment tools will be explored in further detail in part 2.

Formative assessment plays a critical role in the RTI framework, focusing on the component of systems of assessment and data analysis. The formative assessment process helps teachers identify the target, offers multiple opportunities for students to demonstrate their understanding (or lack of understanding), compares their results to the target, evaluates the strengths and weaknesses of the students, and acts on that evaluation. Formative assessments correlated to standards and learning outcomes also provide a cycle of continuous assessment and progress monitoring.

The data from the formative assessments give teachers immediate feedback as to how students are doing in meeting their academic and social goals. Since formative assessments are ongoing, teachers can change strategies immediately and help students improve *during* the learning process rather than waiting for the data from summative assessments at the *end* of the learning process. If teachers use multiple research- and standards-based formative assessment strategies in a systematic way, all students are given a chance to succeed.

However, formative assessments only improve learning when they provide specific feedback to help students achieve deeper understanding and develop critical skills. Feedback of general praise or criticism using phrases such as "good job," "excellent," or "needs more effort" is ineffective. (We will discuss tools for effective feedback in further detail in chapter 5.)

Feedback is powerful when it is targeted at goals and addresses both cognitive and motivational factors at the same time. According to Susan M. Brookhart (2008), author of *How to Give Effective Feedback to Your Students*:

> Good feedback gives students information they need so they can understand where they are in their learning and what to do next—the cognitive factor. Once they feel they understand what to do and why, most students develop a feeling that they have control over their own learning—the motivational factor. (p. 2)

Using the previous scenario, if the teacher presents examples of effective thesis statements, writes some with the class, and provides the checklist to guide struggling students, students know where they are and what to do next. Their cognitive abilities are further enhanced by their self-confidence and their ability to self-assess and monitor their work, motivating them to attempt new challenges.

A teacher must provide more than just feedback. For example, writing, "Your thesis does not contain a controlling idea" on a student's research paper provides feedback, but it also assumes the student knows not only what a controlling idea is but also how to write one. If teachers provide feedback only, students might be able to make the correction on their own—maybe the student knows how to write a controlling idea, but he or she forgot to do it in the paper. However, if the student has no idea how to write a thesis statement with a controlling idea, he or she needs supplemental instruction.

According to Douglas Fisher and Nancy Frey (2010), authors of *Enhancing RTI*, assessment drives instruction and decisions about interventions, and "feedback by itself places the entire responsibility for learning on the student" (p. 113). Feedback that is not accompanied by targeted instruction, differentiated teaching strategies, or cognitive scaffolding will only help students who have the knowledge but simply forgot to use it. It won't help students who never gained that understanding in the first place.

The ultimate feedback at the end of the marking or grading period is a grade. Nothing says you forgot like an F. Unfortunately, there is not a chance for do-overs in summative assessments. Formative assessments, however, foster do-overs and do-betters.

Examples of Formative Assessments

Skillful teachers know how to integrate formative assessments almost seamlessly throughout the lesson. When observing their classrooms, it is often difficult to determine where instruction ends and assessment begins. They introduce a concept or skill in one chunk of instruction and then immediately begin to assess whether or not the students seem to understand it.

One tool that can be used for both instruction and assessment is the K-W-L chart (fig. 2.3), developed by Donna Ogle (1986). Teachers can assign this graphic to individual students or groups of students. Students write all they think they know about a topic in the K column. The teacher can look at the K column to determine which students know a great deal, which students know a few things, and which students need help. The students write what they want to know about the topic in the W column. Students use the L column to list what they have learned about the topic. The K column is similar to a diagnostic assessment; the W column is similar to a formative assessment; and the L column is similar to a summative assessment. This instructional tool also serves as an assessment tool as it gauges where students are and where they need to be.

K	W	L

Figure 2.3: K-W-L chart.

Many diagnostic assessment tools used to collect student data at the beginning of the learning segment can also be used as formative assessment tools that help monitor student progress throughout the learning process. The tools provide data that can be analyzed to determine what strategies are working and what strategies need to be changed. The same tool can be used as a summative assessment at the end of the learning segment to chart the progress of the student. The type of assessment usually depends on its purpose and timing. For example, teachers can use a checklist measuring reading comprehension skills as a diagnostic tool to see how well students understand what they read at the beginning of instruction and then again as formative checkpoints throughout the learning to target specific weaknesses and plan interventions. The same checklist can be used as a summative assessment to show student progress related to the learning goal.

Formative assessments could include more subjective formats such as teacher observations, teacher intuition, and overall impressions, but they are probably more objective and effective when they use a data collection tool like a checklist that allows teachers to collect measurable data, analyze and interpret the results, share with team members, and develop effective interventions to help the student. Figure 2.4 notes some additional formative assessment checklists.

Observation Checklists	Reading Checklists	Group-Work Checklists
Academic skills	Phonics	Peer responses
Social interactions	Fluency	Peer reviews
Behaviors	Comprehension	Social skills
Athletic skills	Response to literature	Leadership skills
Problem-solving abilities	Connections to life, text, self	Team-building skills
Visual/spatial skills		
Oral Communication Checklists	**Written Work Checklists**	**Performance Checklists**
Questioning skills	Practice quizzes	Science projects
Think-pair-share strategy	Rough drafts	Artwork
Speeches	Learning logs	Multimedia presentations
Interviews	Reflective journals	Computer programs
Conferences	Research papers	Music programs
Debates	Math word problems	Drama rehearsals
Mock trials	Graphic organizers	Simulation games
Oral interpretation	Criteria checklists	Performance tasks
Extemporaneous speaking	Analytic rubrics	Portfolio reviews
Socratic seminars		Checklists/rubrics

Figure 2.4: Formative assessment checklists.

These checklists could be labeled as formative assessments because their purpose is to monitor instruction and ascertain students' progress related to learning goals. Since they are administered throughout the learning segment, they are usually not graded. They are typically considered "work in progress," "participation," or "classwork," or if they are graded, they are weighted less than summative grades. Many of these same formative assessments could eventually become summative assessments.

One of the missions of RTI is to use proactive preventions and appropriate interventions to help all students learn. In the past, teachers placed too much emphasis on the summative assessments that occurred at the end of the learning, when it is too late to help the students. Teachers used formative assessments as checkpoints and then created completely different assessments (usually tests) for the final evaluation. Teachers need to shift from using too many summative assessments toward a more balanced approach that uses more formative assessments throughout the learning to provide feedback that helps teachers redirect their teaching and students redirect their learning to meet their goals (Burke, 2010). Figure 2.5 shows how teachers can balance formative assessments and summative assessments to reflect the purpose and timing of the assessment.

Formative Assessment Process		Summative Assessment Process
Assessment *for* Learning		Assessment *of* Learning
Purpose: To provide ongoing feedback to improve learning		Purpose: To evaluate final efforts to prove learning
Timing: During the learning segment		Timing: At the end of the learning segment
Informal teacher questions		Formal oral interview
Conversation with student		Conference with student
Informal observation		Formal observation
Rough drafts of written work		Final copy of written work
Learning log (in progress)		Final learning log entries
Reflective journal (multiple drafts)		Final journal entries
Mathematics problem-solving steps	⟷	Mathematics final solution
Practice science experiment		Final science experiment
Rehearsal of presentation		Final presentation
Working portfolio		Showcase portfolio
Practice checklist for do-overs		Final checklist
Practice rubric		Final rubric
Homework, quiz		Teacher-made test
Benchmark/interim tests		High-stakes standardized test

Figure 2.5: The balanced assessment process.

Source: *Adapted from Burke, 2010, p. 25. Used with permission.*

Feedback plays a critical role in both teaching and learning, and it goes beyond formal testing. Teachers informally assess their students' responses to questions, oral and written work, attitudes, behaviors, and enthusiasm to learn. The feedback generated from this informal data combined with formal assessment data helps teachers develop appropriate curricula and differentiated instructional strategies to meet their students' academic and social needs. By the same token, students use their teachers' informal questions and answers, oral and written comments about their work or behavior, facial expressions, and body language to learn more about how they are doing. When students utilize the constructive feedback provided by these informal formative assessments, they increase their learning and improve their performance on summative assessments. Types of informal feedback are shown in figure 2.6.

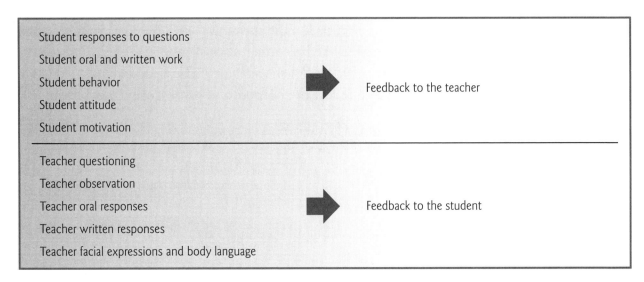

Figure 2.6: Informal feedback.

Common Formative Assessments

Variables related to teachers' instruction and assessment practices create a big problem in collecting assessment data. If each teacher in a grade level at a school decides what to teach, how to teach it, when to teach it, and how to assess it, objectively gauging how each student is doing becomes difficult. Moreover, if each teacher determines his or her own grading scale, a student in one class may exceed the standard but receive a lower grade than a student in the same grade who only met the standard. The expression "comparing apples to oranges" often applies to both formative and summative assessments when teachers create their assessments in isolation.

To combat these problems, many schools and districts work in grade-level, departmental, or vertical teams, or they form professional learning communities to develop common curricula and assessments to ensure that all students have the same educational opportunities. Douglas B. Reeves (2010), founder of the Leadership and Learning Center, believes that "until a school has common formative assessments that provide evidence of common expectations for every student in the same class in the same grade, learning opportunities and expectations will remain wildly varied from one classroom to the next" (p. 71). He states that school leaders need to do more than review lesson-planning notebooks. They need to provide frequent opportunities for teacher teams to establish curriculum content and provide standards-based common formative assessments to measure student growth. The data derived from the common assessments help teachers change their instruction throughout the learning process.

Good teachers assess student learning using a variety of informal and formal assessment tools and strategies, but

> the addition of team-developed common formative assessments to each teacher's assessment arsenal is a powerful weapon, not only for monitoring student learning in a consistent and equitable way, but also for providing each teacher with vital information regarding the effectiveness of his or her instructional strategies. (DuFour, DuFour, Eaker, & Karhanek, 2010, p. 28)

Common formative assessments include the following:

- Selected-response questions (matching, multiple choice)
- Constructed-response questions (essays, fill-in-the-blank)
- Performance tasks
- Checklists
- Rubrics
- Projects
- Portfolios

Teachers should meet in advance of a unit to develop common formative assessments aligned to their state or provincial standards, curriculum, and pacing calendars. These common assessments serve as benchmarks to check how students are doing along the way rather than waiting until the summative assessment at the end when it is too late to help the student.

Formative assessments and common formative assessments both serve as benchmarks; however, common formative assessments ensure a more accurate evaluation, help teachers identify strengths and weaknesses in how they each teach skills and standards, and ensure that the evaluation is equitable (since all students are being evaluated with the same tool and scale). If teachers learn from each other in the process of scoring, and adjust instruction, students in each class have similar learning opportunities, making the curriculum "guaranteed and viable."

Fisher and Frey (2010) believe that common formative assessments "provide teachers with data that spur conversation about instructional and curricular design. They also trigger conversations about students who need supplemental or intensive instruction" (p. 117). Administering common assessments is the beginning of a journey to measure teaching and student learning. Buffum, Mattos, and Weber (2009) believe that "giving a common assessment is not an end in itself, but a means to better measure teaching and student learning" (p. 183). Figure 2.7 shows some critical outcomes and essential questions they believe teacher teams should consider when reviewing common assessment data.

We give common assessments so we can . . .

. . . Identify which students have not demonstrated mastery of essential standard(s). Because we give common assessments to measure student mastery of essential standard(s), common assessments should identify those students who need additional help and support. Additionally, if an assessment measures more than one essential standard, then the test results must provide more than an overall score for each student but also delineate specifically which standards each student did not pass.

Essential Question: Which specific students did not demonstrate mastery?

. . . Identify effective instructional practices. Because our teachers have autonomy in how they teach essential standards, it is vital that common assessment data help validate which practices were effective. This can be done best when common assessment results are displayed in such a way that allows each teacher to compare his or her students' results to other teachers who teach the same course.

Essential Question: Which instructional practices proved to be most effective?

. . . Identify patterns in student mistakes. Besides using common assessment results to identify best instructional practices, these data should also be used to determine ineffective instructional practices. When analyzing the types of mistakes that failing students make, note patterns that point to weaknesses or gaps in the initial instruction.

Essential Question: What patterns can we identify from the student mistakes?

. . . Measure the accuracy of the assessment. Analyze the validity of each test question. Over time, this will build a team's capacity to create better assessments.

Essential Question: How can we improve this assessment?

. . . Plan and target interventions. The ultimate goal of any professional learning community is to ensure high levels of learning for all students. If your team uses common assessments to identify students in need of additional help, determine effective and ineffective instructional practices, and measure the validity of the assessment, you will have the information needed to plan and implement targeted interventions to assist the students that need help.

Essential Question: What interventions are needed to provide failed students additional time and support?

Figure 2.7: Common assessment desired outcomes.

Source: *Buffum, Mattos, & Weber, 2009, p. 183. Used with permission.*

Since it would take a great deal of time and teamwork to develop common assessments for every standard, teams need to focus on the most important standards—the "power standards" that are essential for learning (Reeves, 2010). One example of a power standard is informational writing. The informational writing standard is first introduced in elementary school and is reinforced with increasing levels of difficulty throughout middle school, high school, and college. It is compulsory not only in English but also in science, social studies, psychology, art, music, and any subject that requires students to research a topic and provide information in a written format.

Teams can work across grade levels and content areas to identify the key power standards required in multiple areas. Sometimes teachers from different grade levels create a vertical team to meet and work on the same power standard because it has similar elements in the various grade levels. For example, the higher grade levels may require more descriptors and have a greater level of difficulty, but the purpose and the framework for writing an informational report or research paper are fundamentally the same for grade levels and subject areas.

When teacher teams collaboratively examine the results of their team-made common formative assessments, "they can identify struggling students who need more time and support along the way" (Huff, 2009, p. 39). Assessment is the critical component in determining the effectiveness of any response to intervention.

In Conclusion

Assessment in the 21st century means much more than just giving students a test each Friday, and the days of using only homework and quizzes to determine how a student is doing are over. Today's teachers need to relate to each student by accepting and teaching to his or her cultural differences and learning styles by differentiating their instruction and assessment strategies. Teachers must move beyond pedagogical practices that don't work and adopt research-based strategies that tie their instruction to the academic needs of their students. This process necessitates frequent formative assessments. Linking the results of formative assessments to instructional changes can improve student learning. The "wait to fail" model focused too much on summative assessments that were administered too late in the process to allow improvement. Effective formative assessment shows how students are struggling in real time and allows teachers to take immediate steps to close the gap before the deficit is so large that students will not be able to experience academic or behavioral success.

Author Nancy P. Gallavan (2009) believes that teachers spend most of their time assessing their learners. She says:

> Every time you check to see if your learners understand or "get it," you are conducting an assessment. You assess when you observe activities, listen to discussions, read written responses, view drawn illustrations, watch performances, and pay attention to body

language. You assess before the learning, during the learning, and after the learning; you assess formally and informally, directly and indirectly, by choice and by chance. (p. 6)

Formative assessment is ongoing, and it should be blended almost seamlessly into instruction. In fact, assessment should drive instruction; teachers should begin with the end in mind (standards and curricular goals), planning backward to address curriculum units and instruction.

This is the era of "multiple measurements" and "one size does not fit all." Teachers who use a variety of assessment strategies are able to paint a portrait of a student as a learner rather than taking a snapshot of a student on the day he or she took a test. Learning is fluid, and the uses for assessment are also becoming more fluid.

Chapter 3

Using Assessment Data to Inform Decision Making

Assessment data are the foundation for decision making regarding classroom instruction and practices as well as interventions. Therefore, a clear system of data collection and analysis is crucial to student success in the RTI framework. Effective schools constantly monitor student progress and develop systems that gather data so that the information can be analyzed to increase student learning (Lezotte, 1992). The pages that follow offer techniques that can be incorporated into a systematic process of assessment, data collection, and analysis.

Data Analysis

As mentioned previously, educators use various forms of assessment within an RTI system. However, regardless of the type of assessment, the steps for effective data analysis are the same (see fig. 3.1, page 28): gather the data, graph the information, analyze the results, and act on the findings.

Gather the Data

The responsibility of collecting assessment data falls to different staff members depending on the type of assessment. For example, the district most often collects systemwide universal screening data. Universal screening results provide for the opportunity to compare students within a classroom, within a grade level, and within a district. Common assessment results are collected by those most closely associated with the assessment and often result in practices similar to those of universal screening.

The classroom teacher collects formative and summative assessment data. He or she also needs to record and chart or graph these data—especially teacher-made tests, checklists, and rubric results—to effectively analyze the results. The analyses can be used to change classroom instruction or instructional strategies.

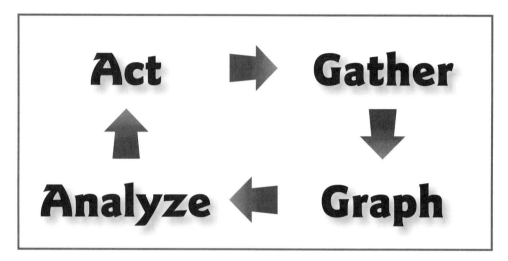

Figure 3.1: Steps for data analysis.

The staff members who provide interventions gather and chart progress-monitoring results. Gathering and graphing should occur within a day of the assessment, as necessary adjustments need to take place well in advance of the next assessment period.

Turnaround time, the period between when the assessment is given and when the teachers receive the results, should be as short as possible for all assessments. The sooner the results can be analyzed, the quicker students with deficits will receive assistance. Computerized assessment systems provide results in a timely fashion and often have valuable ways to report the data instantly.

Data are easiest to manipulate when collected in a digital format. Spreadsheets or electronic gradebooks work well for graphing results. Paper-based gradebooks can be highlighted to visualize patterns, but the ability to manipulate the results is very limited.

Graph the Information

To be of any use, the data must be graphed after they are gathered. Visual representations of data can take many forms, displaying different types of information. (We highlight various ways to create visual representations and report information later in this chapter.) However, several representations are not necessary for a specific set of data. The representation used should provide a revealing picture of the intended or expected results compared with the results actually attained, and student progress should be clearly represented through the organization and display of data (Shores & Chester, 2009).

Choosing the right data representation is dependent on the type and quantity of information being represented. In some cases, a chart may provide enough of a picture. Highlighting techniques can be used with a chart to accentuate trends. Various types of graphs can paint a picture that is difficult to see within a chart. When manipulating the data, the best choice of representation is the one that clearly illustrates meaning. A variety of examples follows.

Analyze the Results

To make the greatest impact on student achievement, each level within the district needs to play a key role in analyzing gathered information. These roles are outlined in table 3.1.

Table 3.1: Data Uses and Users

Key Data Users	Type of Use
District	Universal screening data and common assessment data are analyzed to identify patterns when looking at aggregated and disaggregated groups. Comparisons are made across the district and among schools to discover strengths. Practices resulting in areas of strength are shared across the district. District challenges are identified, and actions are planned to eliminate areas of deficit.
School	Universal screening data and common assessment data are analyzed to identify patterns when looking at aggregated and disaggregated groups. Comparisons are made across grade levels and classrooms to discover strengths. Practices resulting in areas of strength are shared throughout the building. School challenges are identified, and actions are planned to eliminate areas of deficit.
Grade Level or Department	Universal screening data and common assessment data are analyzed to identify patterns when looking at aggregated and disaggregated groups specific to the grade level or subject area. Strengths and challenges are identified. Practices resulting in strengths are shared with others in the department or grade level. Action plans are created to eliminate areas of deficit.
Teacher	Formative assessment data are analyzed to identify group and individual strengths and challenges. Changes in instruction and selection of strategies are made as a result of the data. Continued use of a variety of classroom assessments monitor student growth and knowledge of concepts as they are taught.
Student	Formative assessment results are viewed and analyzed to determine strengths and areas of challenge. Students reflect on the results and identify goals that will help them rise to the next level of success. Younger students will need more support in this process. Students at all levels identify the support needed as they move to the next level of achievement.

Universal screenings should be evaluated at the district and school levels for various purposes. At the district level, the data should reveal how many students have not received the predetermined cut scores, which identify the expected level of success for students who are making adequate progress. For example, if the highest score possible is a 48, but anything over 40 is acceptable, those numbers should be identified in advance. The bar should be set so that students not meeting expectations are identified and progress is further monitored. In addition, scores should be analyzed to determine the percentage of students not achieving expected results. If the scores indicate that more than 20 percent of students need a Tier 2 intervention, further analysis is required.

Districts should also be aware of results obtained at individual schools throughout the district. If differences among schools are noteworthy, further investigation is warranted. Some schools may require additional support or professional development for students to experience greater levels of success at Tier 1. Schools can share their expertise with each other in order to spread best practices throughout the district. Additionally, districts may want to use the data to best meet the needs of all district students, by responding with suggestions for professional development, curriculum alignment, or additional resources.

At the classroom level, educators use formative assessments to determine the level of effectiveness of current instruction and instructional practices. Were the intended results achieved? Were students able to demonstrate understanding of the essential outcomes? Did any of the students struggle with the content or concepts being taught? What instructional decisions should be considered as a result of the data?

Progress-monitoring analysis centers on comparing student progress on skills developed during the intervention with the expected progress. Assessment scores are charted over time so that intervention teams can visualize the progress made throughout the intervention. When analyzing the results, the team should consider the length of time a student has had to make progress in an intervention and compare the current length of time the student is participating in an intervention to the expected "to-date" growth by the end of the intervention. Growth compared to end expectations assists teachers in determining if the intervention is achieving adequate results.

Act on the Findings

After analyzing the results, staff members design next steps to meet student needs. Data may indicate the need for reteaching a concept or component. Some students may be ready for extension activities because of their current depth of understanding. Teachers can vary instructional practices and form flexible student groups to respond to students with similar needs. They can also use the results of the data to inform decisions on the effectiveness of instructional practices.

Before acting on the findings, the following question should be asked: what, if anything, should be done as a result of what the data show? For example, a response would be necessary if the scores on a universal screening indicated a notable discrepancy between a student and grade-level peers. Students who show deficits, but not at the determined level of concern, should be placed on a watch list, and teachers should monitor the formative assessments of those students closely to determine if they are making adequate progress. If there is a lack of adequate progress, educators can change the strategies they use with the student. More intensive interventions may become necessary if strategies are unsuccessful.

When using progress-monitoring assessments, the response to data analysis is dependent on the expected level of growth over a predetermined period of time. If appropriate progress is not evident, the team must decide whether more time in the intervention will promote the needed results or if a different intervention is required.

Formative assessment data create the cornerstone of effective instruction (Brown-Chidsey & Steege, 2005). Actions based on these data typically lead to changes in classroom strategies, diversification of materials, the use of flexible grouping, or other such responses. Fisher and Frey (2010) use the term *informative assessment*, which reflects the idea that assessment results should provide a "rich portrait of student performance" (p. 115). The first response to concerns based on formative assessment data should not be a Tier 2 or 3 intervention. Instead, the appropriate action would be to consider various responses that can take place within the general education classroom. Students who demonstrate a lack of progress over time, after classroom responses have occurred, are likely candidates for interventions at Tier 2. Formative assessment data gathered over time can be used to influence discussion and support actions taken by intervention teams.

Representations and Interpretations of Assessment Data

When evaluating formative assessment results, the data are used to guide next steps. This section highlights graphs and charts that will assist this purpose.

For any classroom assessment, teachers can construct an item analysis, which provides two important pieces of information: (1) it highlights a specific student having difficulties, and (2) it pinpoints the areas of difficulty being experienced by a student, the class, or a portion of the class. Figure 3.2 (page 32) is an item analysis that charts the results of a classroom assessment.

Test item numbers are listed across the top of the page. Teachers indicate incorrect answers by placing a one in the cell. To save time, the auto-fill function on a spreadsheet can be used to place zeros in all empty cells. The last row lists the sums of all incorrect responses in a column, indicating which items students found difficult. For example, these results clearly show that most students struggled with item three. Reteaching the material covered in that item is likely the next logical step.

The last column of the chart shows which students are struggling. Higher numbers indicate more incorrect responses. Teachers can use this chart to create flexible groups of students who struggled with the same concepts. In this case, the same three students were unable to accurately complete items seven, eight, nine, and ten. Ezekial, Marietta, and Justin have demonstrated a need for further support and instruction. Providing these students with more time and experience with the content will lead to a deeper understanding.

Student	#1	#2	#3	#4	#5	#6	#7	#8	#9	#10	Total
Adam	0	0	0	0	0	0	0	0	0	0	0
Ezekial	0	0	1	0	1	0	1	1	1	1	6
Jenny	0	0	0	0	0	0	0	0	0	0	0
Juan	0	0	1	0	0	0	0	0	0	0	1
Maria	0	0	0	0	0	0	0	0	0	0	0
Marjorie	0	0	1	0	0	0	1	0	0	0	2
Sam	0	0	1	0	0	0	0	0	0	0	1
Meghan	0	0	1	0	0	0	0	0	0	0	1
Jordan	0	0	0	0	0	0	0	0	0	0	0
Bart	0	0	0	0	0	0	0	0	0	0	0
Brett	0	0	1	0	0	0	0	0	0	0	1
Marietta	0	0	1	0	0	1	1	1	1	1	6
Joshua	0	0	1	0	0	0	0	0	0	0	1
Donald	0	0	0	0	0	0	0	0	0	0	0
Justin	0	0	1	0	1	0	1	1	1	1	6
Maggie	0	0	1	0	0	0	0	0	0	0	1
Jennifer	0	0	1	0	0	0	0	0	0	0	1
Yolanda	0	0	0	0	0	0	0	0	0	0	0
Morgan	0	0	1	0	0	0	0	0	0	0	1
Item Totals	0	0	12	0	2	1	4	3	3	3	

Figure 3.2: Example item analysis.

Involving students in data analysis can provide important insights into next steps for instruction. Graphs of formative assessment results like figure 3.3 can be shared with the students so they are aware of how the class performed. In figure 3.3, it is clear that a high number of students struggled with number three. The class could provide insights into why this particular question was more difficult for them. In a case like this, student input is extremely valuable as students are likely to provide information that will be beneficial to the teacher during the reteaching phase of instruction.

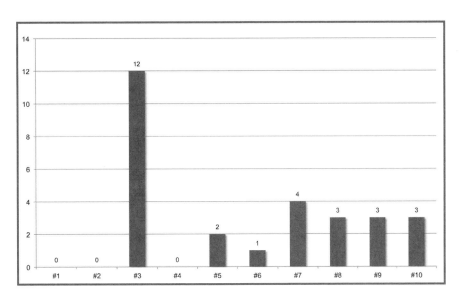

Figure 3.3: Number of incorrect responses by question.

Figure 3.4 (page 34) illustrates the results of a rubric. A rubric identifies the criteria important to the successful completion of a product or performance (see chapter 7 for more detailed information about rubrics). Students are made aware of the criteria then evaluated according to those criteria. In this case, student writing was critiqued in the categories of ideas, organization, word choice, voice, sentence fluency, and conventions. The rubric itself contained descriptors of quality for each criterion. Students could score a 1, 2, 3, or 4, with 4 being highest on this rubric.

Each row in figure 3.4 shows the results achieved by an individual student, the average score, and the total score. This rubric offers a total possible score of 24. The results as indicated in this format clearly identify strengths and challenges.

Student names are listed down the left side of the spreadsheet, and rubric categories or criteria are along the top row. The rubric items that were difficult for the entire group become apparent when scanning the totals listed in the second to last row; the lower the score, the more the students struggled with the item. Teachers can easily identify the struggling students by viewing the last column; lower scores indicate struggling students. The last column of data also shows which students are proficient or exceptional writers.

By reviewing the results in this format, the teacher can quickly see the need to provide additional instruction and practice in the area of sentence fluency. Its average of 1.79 is the lowest of all evaluated areas. Although a few students received a score of 3, the majority scored 1 or 2. Additional writing opportunities as well as differentiated lessons and assignments will be helpful to address whole-group needs.

	Ideas	Organization	Word Choice	Voice	Sentence Fluency	Conventions	Average	Total
Bart	2	2	2	4	1	1	2.00	12
Maria	3	1	1	4	1	2	2.00	12
Jennifer	4	2	3	3	1	1	2.33	14
Morgan	4	1	2	4	2	1	2.33	14
Yolanda	3	1	3	3	1	3	2.33	14
Donald	3	2	3	3	1	3	2.50	15
Brett	3	4	2	3	2	3	2.83	17
Ezekial	4	2	3	3	2	3	2.83	17
Juan	4	1	3	3	3	3	2.83	17
Marietta	3	3	2	4	2	3	2.83	17
Marjorie	3	3	3	3	2	3	2.83	17
Jenny	4	2	2	3	3	4	3.00	18
Justin	3	3	3	4	2	3	3.00	18
Maggie	4	3	4	4	2	1	3.00	18
Meghan	3	2	4	4	2	3	3.00	18
Adam	4	4	4	2	2	3	3.17	19
Sam	4	2	4	4	1	4	3.17	19
Joshua	4	2	4	4	2	4	3.33	20
Jordan	4	3	4	4	2	4	3.50	21
Item Totals	66	43	56	66	34	52		
Item Averages	3.47	2.26	2.95	3.47	1.79	2.74		

Figure 3.4: Writing rubric results.

A bar graph can be used in various ways to represent and interpret assessment results. Using the same rubric scenario, figure 3.5 provides a visual of the average results listed by criterion and can be used to analyze group performance. The graph clearly shows that the group struggled most with sentence fluency, indicating a need for additional instruction and application in this area.

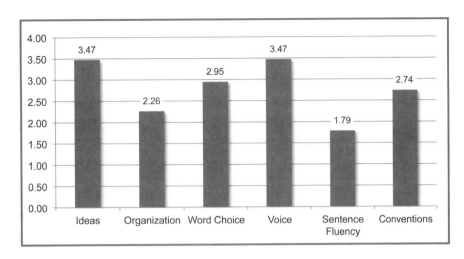

Figure 3.5: Item averages.

Rubric results can also be graphed by individual students (see fig. 3.6). Teachers can share this type of visual with the students to help them interpret their results and reflect on steps necessary to enhance their performance. For example, if Bart were looking at his results, he would realize that his greatest areas of need are sentence fluency and conventions. He might set a goal to be more conscious of grammar and spelling and ask a friend or parent to help him edit his work. Such a graphic representation is also beneficial for students who have difficulty identifying areas of strength. Bart would also notice from the results that he achieved the highest level of performance in voice. This is an area of celebration. Feedback regarding both strengths and challenges causes students to better evaluate their own performance. In doing so, they will realize not only what they need to improve but also what they need to continue.

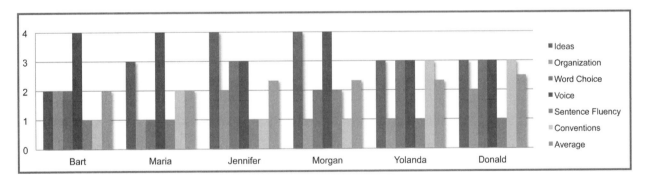

Figure 3.6: Rubric results by student.

Rubric results can also be graphed by trait (see fig. 3.7, page 36). Such a visual is valuable during instructional planning and in the creation of flexible groups. In viewing the criteria and student results in this way, teachers can easily see which students have similar needs. For example, Maria, Morgan, and Yolanda could be placed in a flexible group created to reinforce concepts related to the organizational aspects of writing.

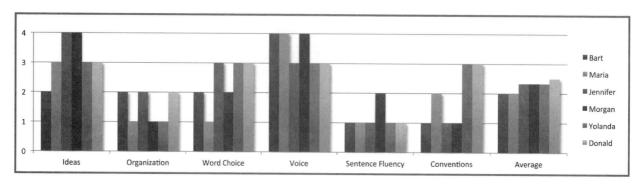

Figure 3.7: Rubric results by trait.

Progress-monitoring data represent an individual student's growth while engaged in a specific form of instruction or intervention. Figures 3.8 and 3.9 illustrate student responses to a reading intervention and a behavioral intervention. The visual representation of progress-monitoring data is meaningful to both the teacher and student. Actually being able to see the progress or lack thereof provides a deeper level of understanding than does a list of numbers. The graphs essentially tell the stories of student progress.

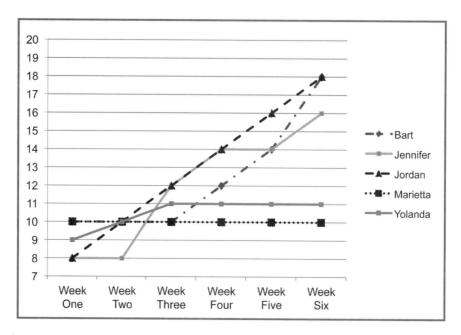

Figure 3.8: Words per minute attained on weekly reading assessment.

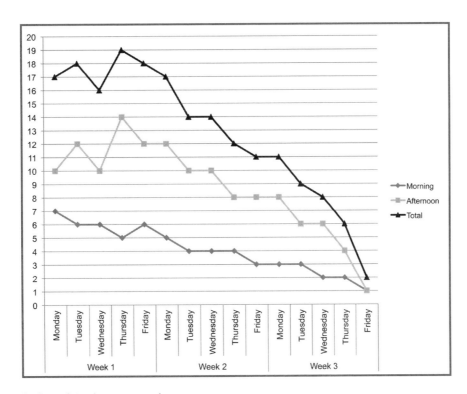

Figure 3.9: Record of Randy's classroom outbursts.

Subject-area records can provide a picture of progress as well. Figure 3.10 is a graph of math assessment results. When viewing the graph, a teacher is able to see which students are making adequate progress, which students are surpassing expectations, and which students require additional attention in order to experience success.

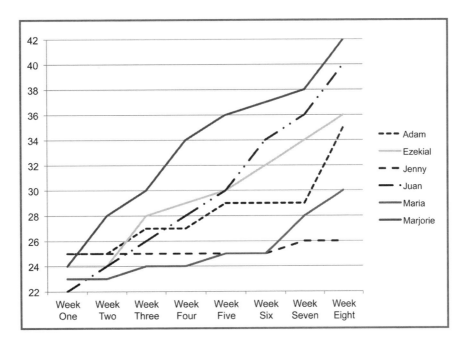

Figure 3.10: Weekly results on math assessments.

Disaggregation of data is a necessary part of any survey of large-scale data, including universal screening data and common assessment data. Constituent parts often include gender, ethnicity, socioeconomic status, and special education status, as well as any other demographics important to the district (see fig. 3.11).

Unlike classroom assessment data, which can be used to make immediate changes in classroom instruction, district data enable patterns to emerge, and multiple snapshots are needed to determine whether the data require a call to action. Districts respond to patterns by analyzing the cause and creating plans to eliminate score discrepancies and deficiencies. Without this analysis and action, districts would not make the gains necessary to boost student success on a larger scale.

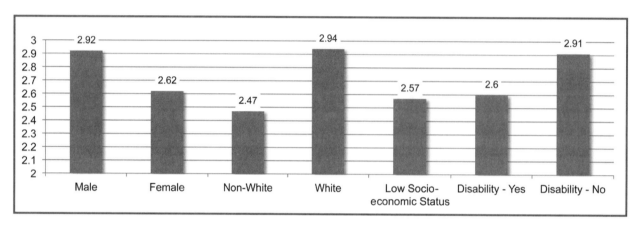

Figure 3.11: Disaggregation of a writing assessment's average rubric scores.

Deciding to Act

Assessment results should be followed by high-quality corrective instruction (Guskey, 2007). However, before an educator can act, he or she must decide what actions to take. The following questions will help guide educators and groups of educators in viewing classroom, school, and district data and determining the best course of action.

Questions to be posed by the *teacher* following formative assessments:

- According to the data, what are the group's strengths?

- According to the data, what are the group's challenges?

- What large-group instructional support is needed as a result of the challenges?

- Which individuals are in need of additional support and for what reasons?

- What small-group or individual support is needed as a result of the challenges?

Questions to be posed by *schools* following common assessments:

- According to the data, what are the school's strengths? Are the strengths tied to specific grade levels or subjects?

- Are particular strategies being used that result in the strengths? How can such strategies be shared?

- According to the data, what group or subject-area challenges are evident?

- Are there differences in the performances of disaggregated groups?

- Are there differences in the performances of grade levels?

- Are there patterns of challenges between this data and previous data?

Questions to be posed by the *district* following common assessments:

- According to the data, what strengths are evident? Are the strengths tied to specific schools or subjects?

- Are particular strategies being used that result in the strengths? How can such strategies be shared across the district?

- According to the data, what group or subject-area challenges are evident?

- Are there differences in the performances of disaggregated groups?

- Are there differences in the performances of grade levels?

- Are there differences in the performances of schools?

- Are there patterns of challenges between these data and previous data?

- Can current initiatives be linked to a positive impact on student performance?

A response to assessment data is needed with each analysis. This might require something as simple as a change in strategy or something more sophisticated, like a change in programming at the district level. With each action, a measurement of success is needed to determine the impact of the action. Lack of action is not acceptable if student achievement is to be impacted.

In Conclusion

Assessment results create the foundation for informed instructional decisions (Hoover, 2009), and a system of assessment analysis is needed to create a situation of continuous improvement.

When working within the RTI framework in an effort to positively impact student achievement, educators should follow these steps to ensure effective data analysis:

1. Gather the data.

2. Graph the information.

3. Analyze the results.

4. Act on the findings.

These steps create an unending cycle. After acting on the findings, data need to be collected and analyzed so that one can determine the impact of the actions taken. This continuous cycle will lead to the use of practices and procedures that lead to positive student results.

Chapter 4
Putting It All Together

The previous chapters have included pieces of the RTI/formative assessment puzzle. Now we need to put those pieces together to create a complete system that promotes student achievement and a successful outcome for increased numbers of students.

To ensure a high degree of success, administrators need to create a system of training, support, and implementation within an RTI framework. That system is illustrated in figure 4.1 (page 42).

Develop a Clear Understanding of the RTI Framework

The RTI framework promotes a common realization of and commitment to a focus on student success. It is through this framework that the essential nature of the assessment process can be understood.

Administrators must provide their teachers with the information they need in order to understand the RTI framework, its purpose, and its potential impact. This can be accomplished through staff development. Learning and implementing new techniques in assessment, data collection, and analysis is an ongoing process.

Teaching Strategies and Formative Assessment

If the implementation of RTI is to succeed, it cannot be assumed that the current understanding of formative assessment practices and current teaching strategies is enough to create a successful outcome. Without new learning, current practices will continue unchanged. That is not to say that current practices are ineffective, but without change, the same results will appear and progress will be halted. If the bank of teaching strategies and formative assessments is to grow, professional development is needed.

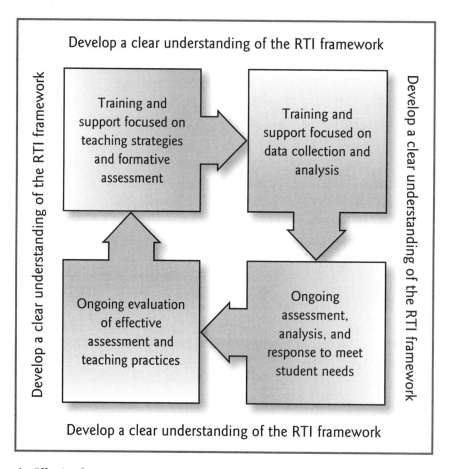

Figure 4.1: The cycle: Effective formative assessment in an RTI framework.

The implementation of new practices should be supported and encouraged through conversation and collaboration. A discussion of the impact of specific formative assessment tools will increase the likelihood of their use. It can no longer be assumed that individual tests are a measure of educational quality (Reeves, 2004). Multiple measures provide both indicators that lead to changing instructional practices and a balanced analysis of educational practices.

Data Collection and Analysis

Data collection and analysis are required steps in the RTI process. Through analyses, teachers can identify and respond to students' needs as part of a systematic approach to promote student success. The tools highlighted in part 2 will help with this process. Data collection and analysis are more likely to occur if time is provided to learn about and implement a variety of data collection tools. These tools need to be meaningful and convenient, and analysis should occur regularly. The result of an effective analysis is the careful consideration of what instructional lessons, methods, or assessments need to change so that increased learning can occur. This analysis will identify what is working and what is not, what to continue and what to eliminate.

Ongoing Assessment, Analysis, and Response

Clearly the most crucial aspect of RTI is responding effectively to student needs. By using data to compare a student to other students, and the student to self, the teacher can create a picture of that student's strengths and challenges and thus respond with actions that can have a positive impact on student success. Such actions have the potential of increasing the number of students who are successful at Tier 1, resulting in fewer students requiring Tier 2 and 3 interventions.

The following chapters include a variety of formative assessment tools that can provide a comprehensive view of students' levels of achievement. However, such a view is not to be just a snapshot; to be effective, assessment, analysis, and response must be a continuous cycle.

Evaluations of Effective Assessment and Teaching Practices

Assessment strategies and teaching practices should be evaluated using data. Do the data support the continued use of the assessment strategy or teaching practice? Does a strategy result in an increased rate of student success? Teachers should analyze assessment results to study the impact of the assessment tools and classroom strategies used and, if warranted, to make changes that increase understanding.

The System in Action

Mrs. Stewbush, principal of New Day Elementary School, wishes to promote the RTI framework within her school and orchestrates a series of professional development opportunities for her staff. During these sessions, she explains the RTI framework, concentrating on the tiers, assessment, data, and record-keeping. She explains that RTI fits naturally with their already-established continuous-improvement process. She then provides teachers with the opportunity for input, and together they discuss details of what the model will look like in their school.

Knowing that increasing awareness and understanding of a variety of teaching strategies and methods of assessment are important, Mrs. Stewbush provides a structure in which new learning can occur. Time is set aside each week for teachers to collaborate and share practices they find beneficial in their classrooms. Some teachers attend conferences and bring back information to share with others. The teachers use a variety of assessment practices and identify some assessments that they will use in common. Data-gathering techniques are shared. Teachers analyze their data and find time to collectively share insights into each other's data. All teachers continue learning through conferences, reading, and sharing.

The teachers at New Day are very aware that all of the new learning will not make a difference if they don't use the information gathered through data analysis and respond to meet the needs of their students. Therefore, they change strategies, implement new practices, and continue to measure student understanding through a variety of assessment tools.

Through their continuous analyses and collaborative conversation, the teachers recognize that some practices are more effective than others and gain an understanding of the methods that appear to have a deeper impact on student understanding. They also understand that it is necessary to eliminate ineffective tools and practices.

Although Mrs. Stewbush started the RTI process in her school, her teachers make it successful. The students benefit as a result of the teachers' cycle of assessment, analysis, and action.

In Conclusion

RTI is a system that can improve student performance with quality teaching strategies and effective assessment practices. Through the use of a variety of assessment tools, the collection and analysis of data, and the evaluation of the success of each instrument, the pathway to improved student success becomes clear.

Strategies and practices that have a positive impact on student achievement need to be duplicated. It's important for administrators to provide collaboration time so that effective practices can be shared among teachers. Institutionalizing positive practices requires time, professional development, and an expectation that practices include assessment tools that have the best results relative to levels of student success. Communication, collaboration, and culture are important components of changing the ordinary way of doing things (DuFour & Eaker, 1998). Change needs to be embedded, not simply initiated.

Part 2

Formative Assessment Tools

Chapter 5

Feedback and Reflection

Feedback and reflection are important components of any learning process. Feedback from the teacher gives students information about their current level of performance compared to the expected level of performance. Feedback also helps students better understand the steps necessary to perform at and achieve a higher level of success. Feedback from the students helps the teacher identify the students' comfort level with the content and provides an indication of the next steps needed to respond to learner needs.

Reflection requires students to consider their performance as compared to the expected level of performance. They then determine what effort, new learning, or assistance is needed to attain a higher level of performance.

Both feedback and reflection are formative in nature. The intent of both is to guide students to increased levels of academic or behavioral success. As a result, feedback and reflection play an important role in RTI.

Types of Feedback

Both the teacher and student play important roles in providing information that can have a positive impact on student achievement. Teachers can react to a student's product or performance by analyzing and comparing it to the expected result. By sharing their observations with the student, they provide direction and next steps that are beneficial to the student. The student can provide the teacher with feedback about his or her level of understanding. This feedback helps the teacher determine the actions that need to be taken to respond to the student's needs appropriately. The sections that follow will provide examples of both teacher and student feedback.

Teacher Feedback

Teacher feedback is the process of providing a student with a reaction to his or her product, performance, or behavior. Its purpose is to impact future occurrences in a positive way. The content of the feedback is of primary importance if the student is to grow from the response. Feedback requires accuracy and honesty. Students need to know what went well and where improvement is required. Feedback should state factually what is, compare it to what should be, and help the student understand the difference while providing guidance to adjust future actions. Through proper feedback, students will have a better chance at overcoming their deficits and accomplishing the next level of success.

Grades and comments like "good job" and "nice work" are not feedback because they give no indication of next steps and do not compare performance to expectation in a way that can be used by a student to improve performance. Effective feedback not only helps students understand how they have performed but also indicates what they need to improve in future performances (Reeves, 2004). Teachers need to involve students in the feedback and assessment process and help them understand that when feedback is given, action is required. Students should use the feedback to improve their level of performance (O'Connor, 2009).

Effective feedback has several characteristics (see fig. 5.1). Feedback needs to be timely. If students are to experience the greatest effect, they need to receive feedback on the first assignment prior to completing the next assignment. For example, if a student works on a math assignment on Monday, and the Tuesday assignment covers the same content, the student needs to understand the quality and accuracy of Monday's assignment prior to starting the new work. If guidance is not given, the same errors will continue, and the student will likely not understand what type of improvement is required. In addition, students may learn and practice erroneous procedures if misunderstandings are not corrected.

Feedback should be:

- Related to the language of the standard
- Timely
- Correlated to curricular goals
- Specific to one or two elements
- Understandable to the students
- Ongoing and consistent
- Offered constructively
- Unbiased
- Objective
- Given with opportunities to improve the work
- Honest
- Ungraded
- Accompanied by appropriate support

Figure 5.1: Characteristics of feedback.

Ongoing and consistent feedback gives students the best chance at a high level of success. Teacher support and direction allow students to better understand the modifications needed for deeper learning and enhanced performance. When assessment results are analyzed, teachers should identify the gap between the expected and actual performance to determine what progress has been made and where further growth is needed (Hoover, 2009). Teachers should then share their analyses with the students.

Effective feedback is honest feedback. A clear and accurate picture of student performance is necessary. Effort should not impact the content of the feedback in a way that skews accuracy, but effort can be recognized for its own merit. If Jennifer is a wonderful student who tries really hard, the feedback still compares her product or performance with the intended outcome and points out the achievements and discrepancies. But the teacher can certainly recognize that Jennifer is a hard worker and tell her so. Not all students realize that effort is an important component of learning and has a direct impact on results. Students can benefit by learning the association between effort and achievement (Marzano, Pickering, & Pollock, 2001).

Student Feedback

Teachers are experts at understanding the classroom and getting a feel for students' levels of understanding by observing and interacting with them. The best way, however, to gain a level of confidence about student understanding is to ask the students. There are a variety of methods to help the students communicate their levels of understanding with the teacher throughout the class period. Instant feedback tools help teachers adjust instruction immediately to meet the needs of the majority of students.

Tools and Methods for Feedback

Although effective, providing feedback can be time consuming for the teacher. However, there are methods and tools to provide feedback in a time-efficient manner. Such tools are highlighted in the following sections and can be used with any grade level.

Rubrics

Rubrics provide meaningful feedback and direction to the students and do not require one-on-one conversations. Rubric scoring can take place in a timely manner because the criteria are well outlined and the descriptors eliminate the need for extensive written comments. Although rubrics are most often completed by teachers, parents and students can complete rubrics as well. If criteria are understood and descriptors are well written, students are very capable of analyzing their own work and the work of others in the classroom. Small groups of students can analyze the work of the group. The class can conduct an analysis on products created during previous years, allowing for a clear understanding of the rubric before they begin their own work. In addition, parents gain a deeper understanding of their child's strengths and challenges when they complete a rubric about a product generated by their child.

Checklists

Feedback checklists are an efficient and effective way to provide students with comments appropriate to future success. This type of checklist is composed of common comments generated by the teacher. The teacher checks the comments related to the student's work and attaches the list to the product. Figures 5.2 and 5.3 are examples of feedback checklists. The expectation is that students read the feedback, make the necessary changes, and resubmit their work. Checklists provide a viable alternative to extensive, repeated written comments.

The area(s) checked requires additional attention.	
Show all work associated with the solution to the problem.	
Include a label to identify your answer.	
Explain how you got your answer.	
Organize your work.	
Check the solution for accuracy.	

Figure 5.2: Feedback checklist for a math task.

The area(s) checked requires additional attention.	
A topic sentence needs to be added or rewritten.	
Information and supporting details need to be added for increased clarity.	
A closing sentence needs to be added or rewritten.	
More descriptive words need to be used.	
More transitions need to be added to connect ideas.	
Conventions require additional attention. Circle all that apply: punctuation, spelling, grammar, capitalization	

Figure 5.3: Feedback checklist for a descriptive writing assignment.

Table Tents

Students can provide feedback to the teacher without direct communication. Table tents in stoplight colors are one example of such a method. Students are provided with small red, yellow, and green table tents. During whole-group instruction, the students change their table tent color, when asked, to reflect their state of mind. Teachers adjust content and speed to respond to student input. Figure 5.4 provides a sample explanation of the colors of this tool.

Table Tent Color	Purpose of Color
Green	I understand! Keep going.
Yellow	I think I understand. Proceed with caution.
Red	You lost me!

Figure 5.4: Table tent feedback.

Whiteboards

Individual student whiteboards are another tool that can be used to gain immediate responses from students. The teacher supplies each student with a small whiteboard and marker and then asks a question appropriate to the class content. Each student writes a response on his or her whiteboard. Teachers indicate when students should hold up the board to show their answers. By simply glancing around the room, it becomes apparent to the teacher which, if any, students are struggling. If necessary, the teacher can respond immediately through a shift in instruction or use of a different instructional technique. A quick think-pair-share, during which students pair up and share their thoughts on the question, may clarify any misunderstandings.

Exit Slips

Exit slips are another popular method for obtaining student feedback. Used in a variety of ways, their purpose is to give the teacher the information needed to plan for class the next day. Figures 5.5 through 5.7 (page 52) provide examples.

Exit Slip	Mrs. Murray's Math Class	Date
The important points from today's class are:		
I am confused about:		

Figure 5.5: Sample exit slip for math class.

Exit Slip	Mr. Smith's Reading Class	Date
Today I learned:		
I think I need help with:		

Figure 5.6: Sample exit slip for reading class.

Exit Slip	Mrs. Shimm's First-Grade Class		Date
After class today:			
☺	☺ ☺	☺ ☺ ☺	☺ ☺ ☺ ☺
I'm really confused.	I need a little help.	I understand.	I could teach this to my friends.

Figure 5.7: Sample exit slip for first-grade class.

Check-Ins

Individual check-ins provide an excellent opportunity for feedback. Check-ins are one- to two-minute miniconferences. A good goal is to have a check-in with each student at least once a week. This would likely require using ten minutes per class as conference time. Students who are experiencing problems may require additional check-ins each week. Teachers may have a predetermined question to ask, or they may simply check in with the student and watch him or her work on the current task.

To make the best use of time, teachers go to the students, instead of asking the students to come to them. In this way, students do not need to interrupt their work to make their way to the teacher's desk. Also, as the teacher makes his or her way to the student, he or she is able to see several students as they are working, not just the few who are part of the check-in group for that day.

Teachers should keep a record of check-in data throughout the year. Teachers who have multiple classes in a day will find this strategy useful to ensure that each student has individual teacher contact at least once a week. The check-in record is an organized, efficient way to complete and monitor feedback sessions. An example of a daily check-in record sheet can be viewed in table 5.1.

Feedback can take multiple forms. The purpose is to provide students with a clear picture of their current status compared to the learning goal and to help them visualize the path leading to successfully achieving the goal. It is important that feedback be genuine and not just a form of praise (Shores & Chester, 2009). Students need to have clear and current knowledge of what success looks like. Feedback has the potential to help students attain a higher level of achievement at all tiers, yet when used consistently at Tier 1, there is a likelihood that fewer students will require a Tier 2 intervention.

Reflection

Reflection necessitates an introspective look at one's own performance. In the classroom, reflection translates to the student looking at his or her current performance and determining the steps necessary to achieve the next level of quality or depth. This process helps students own their learning and set goals for their commitment to the acquisition of knowledge. This process can start with very young children and continue through high school and even life.

Table 5.1: Daily Check-In Record Sheet

	Week One: Problem solving using multiplication					Week Two: Problem solving using multiplication and division				
	Mon.	Tues.	Wed.	Thurs.	Fri.	Mon.	Tues.	Wed.	Thurs.	Fri.
Dale	3					3				
Elissa	3					3				
Ellen	3					3				
Evan	1	2	3				3			
James		3					3			
Jordan		3					3			
Juan			4					4		
Latoya			4					4		
Maria				3				3		
Meghan				2	3				3	
Natalie					3				3	
Nate					3					3
Regina					3					3

1 = minimal understanding; 2 = basic understanding; 3 = proficient understanding; 4 = advanced understanding

Peter Senge (2000) of MIT defines reflection as a spiral in which students produce a product, acquire feedback, and make changes based on that feedback. The change takes place, more feedback is given, and the process is repeated throughout the learning.

Within the RTI framework, teachers desire to have as many students as possible succeed at Tier 1. The greater number of students who succeed in the general education classroom, the fewer interventions needed. When students take responsibility as a key partner in the learning process, the stakes are higher for them personally and their commitment and efforts are increased.

Reflection in conjunction with feedback has the potential of powerfully impacting learning. When reviewing assessment results, students need the ability to reflect on their performance so they can read and interpret the results as well as determine next steps and act on their findings (Stiggins, 2007).

Reflection is not time consuming, yet time needs to be devoted to it. Reflection doesn't happen accidentally; it needs to be planned. Time for reflection can be built into the school day. For example, teachers can generate reflective questions to inspire thought and action. Spending just minutes each day in reflection will help students learn to review their strengths and challenges and determine what response is required to make academic and behavioral gains.

Tools for Reflection

Tools used to encourage student reflection can range from graphic organizers to a set of simple questions—any item that can be used to record thoughts, ideas, or responses to specific prompts. Several examples are provided in the sections that follow.

Graphic Organizers

Graphic organizers provide a useful framework when recording reflections. For example, figures 5.8 through 5.12 (pages 54–57) are designed to help students consider their current performance, strengths, and challenges while determining the next steps for their academic growth. Every tool listed here can be used within any subject area. Some can also be used to analyze behavior. Figures 5.8 and 5.9 can reflect on either academics or behavior.

☼ Reflection on Class Today	
If I could have today back again, what would I do . . .	
The same?	Differently?

Figure 5.8: Reflection on the day.

After completing a project, students fill out a reflective tool to evaluate what they would do differently to increase their level of success (see fig. 5.10).

Students can also use graphic organizers to reflect on and record their goals. Ideally, a goal will be based on a challenge, yet a strength will be used to achieve the goal and eliminate the challenge. Teachers may want students to include a statement about their reflection mentioning the assistance that is required from the teacher. Figure 5.11 (page 56) is specifically used as a record of a student's goal. The goal can be based on something the student wants to learn or a behavior he or she wants to change. Steps are included as a plan to achieve the goal. Teachers should provide direction in monitoring the goal throughout the time frame for which it is intended as well as time for goal reviews and updates.

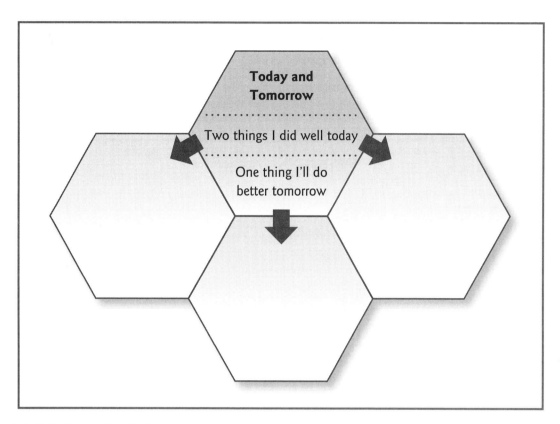

Figure 5.9: Reflection and projection.

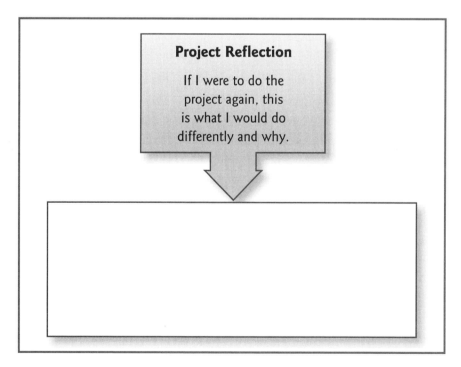

Figure 5.10: Project reflection.

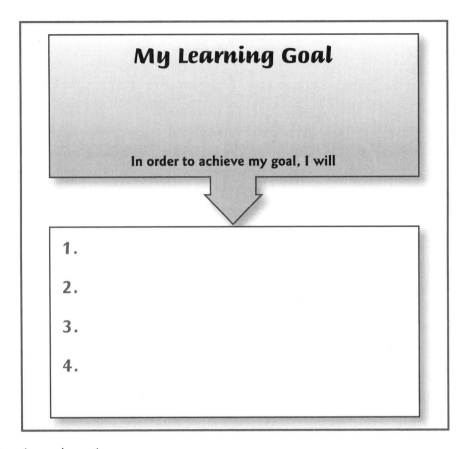

Figure 5.11: Learning goal organizer.

Reflective Exercises

A reflective exercise will result in the growth of understanding by requiring students to consider what they know, determine the questions they have, and establish a plan to gain the knowledge they need to be successful. Teachers can promote reflective exercises prior to completing an assignment, encouraging students to consider the path they will take toward a successful outcome. Reflective questions might include the following:

1. What am I being asked to do?

2. What supplies, materials, or help do I need to accomplish the task?

3. How will I proceed to achieve a successful outcome? How much time is required?

When students take a few extra minutes to preplan their work, the number of successful, timely outcomes will likely increase because they have considered what they need to achieve the desired end. It is similar to planning a trip prior to getting into the car. The end is clearer; needs have been predetermined; and if assistance is required, there is a plan in place to obtain it.

A pattern of daily reflective exercises can be accomplished using limited class time. There are several brief approaches that a teacher can take to promote reflection. A common reflective approach is the think-pair-share model. Students consider their response to a question, pair with a member of the class, and share their responses. Reflection is promoted in that students gain a better understanding of their knowledge level.

Figures 5.12 and 5.13 (page 58) are exercises that can increase student reflection time and also help teachers reflect on next steps for instruction.

Learn—Question—Apply

Two key things I learned in class today:

1.

2.

One question from class today:

One way I can apply what I learned from class today:

Figure 5.12: Learn, question, apply.

Students can work in small groups or independently to reflect on five key pieces of information or processes learned during class. The "five things learned" organizer, shown in figure 5.14 (page 58), is used to record the thoughts generated.

Students can also connect what they already know to their analysis of what next steps are needed to learn at a deeper level. Figure 5.15 (page 59) provides a tool for that purpose.

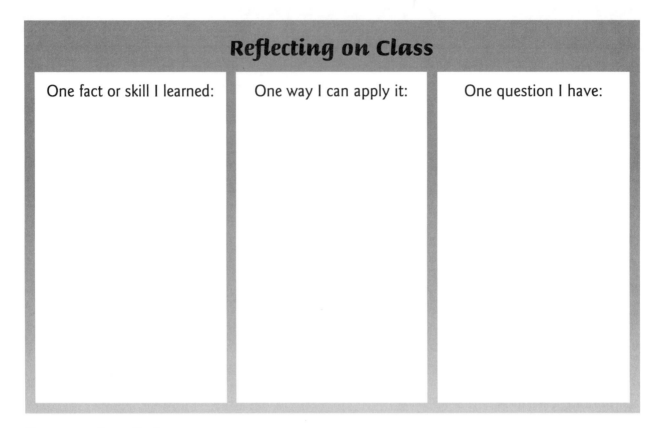

Figure 5.13: Class reflection.

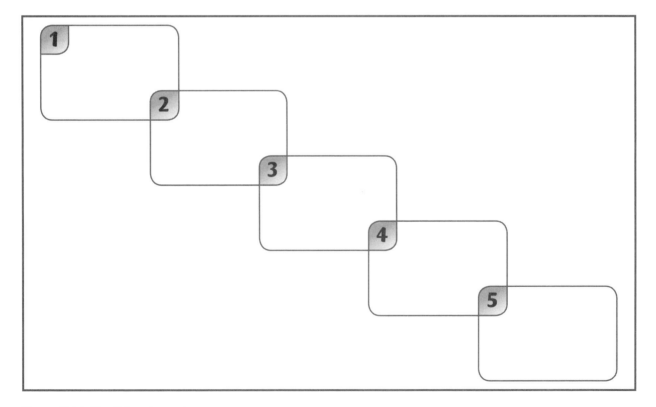

Figure 5.14: Five things learned.

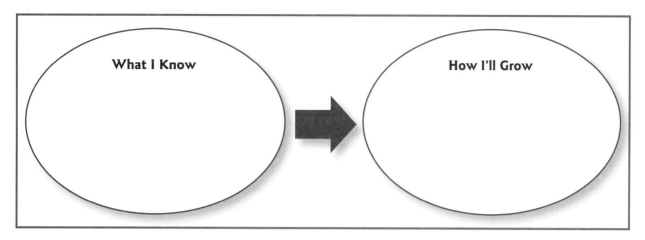

Figure 5.15: Know and grow.

Class time can be used for verbal reflections as well. Teachers ask students to consider what they know, identify what they are unsure of, and project the next steps to promote student success. Verbal reflection can take place during the last few minutes of class, when all students can share a key learning concept from class. One at a time, students share their thoughts orally until time runs out or all students have shared. Or students can work with a partner or small group to hear the reflections of others and share their own. It is through reflections that students have the opportunity to be introspective, analytical, and visionary. When students are given the time to analyze their knowledge, skills, and ability to apply what they have learned, they are better able to prepare for the next steps associated with achieving success.

In Conclusion

In an RTI structure, student success is directly related to the outcomes necessary to achieve a solid academic or behavioral performance. Whether providing feedback or promoting reflection, the goal is to do the following:

1. Analyze the student's current performance or level of understanding.

2. Compare where the student is to the required level of performance or goal.

3. Understand and share the steps necessary to close the gap between what is and what needs to be if the student is to experience success.

4. Take action to acquire the desired level of understanding.

The RTI framework provides a structure that supports student achievement in both academics and behavior. The foundation of the framework relies on research-based classroom practices with an emphasis on assessment, including the formative assessment process. The strategies and tools highlighted provide teachers with a variety of options to better understand, measure, and evaluate student growth. As a result, student needs can be identified and addressed in a timely fashion, possibly limiting the need for further intervention.

Chapter 6

Checklists for Learning

Atul Gawande, best-selling author of *The Checklist Manifesto: How to Get Things Right* (2010), believes that avoidable failures consistently plague us in health care, government, the law, the financial industry, and almost every realm of organized activity. He says that people have accumulated know-how and have nurtured highly skilled, highly trained, and hardworking employees to accomplish extraordinary things. Nevertheless, avoidable failures are common because the knowledge is often unmanageable. He says the volume and complexity of what people know have exceeded their ability to deliver knowledge's benefits correctly, safely, and reliably. Gawande (2010) believes

> we need a different strategy for overcoming failure, one that builds on experience and takes advantage of the knowledge people have but somehow also makes up for our inevitable human inadequacies. And there is such a strategy—though it will seem almost ridiculous in its simplicity, maybe even crazy to those of us who have spent years carefully developing ever more advanced skills and technologies. It is a checklist. (p. 13)

Checklists are graphic organizers that help people complete steps in a logical and sometimes sequential manner. Some students are capable of completing a project independently by analyzing what has to be done, formulating a plan, executing the plan, evaluating the outcomes, and reflecting on their own performance. Other students, however, require some help with the problem-solving process.

One of the core concepts of RTI is to monitor student progress with ongoing data to see if students have mastered each step in the lesson. Author Mike Schmoker (2011) states:

> As students practice, and between each step in the lesson, the teacher should conduct "formative assessment" by checking—assessing—to see how many students have mastered that particular step. This ongoing "check for understanding" allows the teacher to

see what needs to be clarified or explained in a different way to slow down, or when it's all right to speed up the pace of the lesson. (p. 54)

Checklists help teachers check for understanding and provide continuous assessment and progress monitoring to all students in Tier 1 and to targeted students in Tiers 2 and 3. Teachers use oral and written comments on checklists to provide immediate feedback to help struggling students before they fall too far behind.

Checklists in the RTI Framework

The purpose of formative assessment and the RTI framework is to catch deficiencies early enough in the learning process to change instructional tactics and intensify the remediation as needed. Checklists provide the formative feedback to facilitate this process.

Checklists provide clear guidelines and specific feedback to all students, but they can be particularly effective for struggling students. Some students don't think logically; some have ineffective organizational skills. When teachers give verbal directions about how to complete assignments, some students don't pay attention or have difficulty following the directions because they don't understand the vocabulary or concepts. When teachers give written directions, which are usually in prose, some students have trouble reading or comprehending abstract ideas used in technical or informational writing and are not able to understand what they are being asked to do. Verbiage can get in the way of understanding, and students with weak verbal skills tend to get confused when teachers use mostly lecture methods or assign readings that contain difficult vocabulary and concepts. To compound the problem, students become frustrated or discouraged when they don't know what questions to ask when they seek help.

Fisher and Frey (2010) believe teachers can use checklists as a simple instrument for capturing a snapshot of students' evolving skills. They discuss how a checklist to assess students' understanding of math skills, for example, can be used to facilitate conversations between the classroom teacher and the supplemental and intensive intervention teachers as well as between classroom teachers and parents. They explain, "When checklists are used in this manner, they become a critical component of the assessment system from which teachers can draw to effectively implement RTI" (p. 101). Checklists provide a user-friendly method of translating the often vague and abstract standards-based language and concepts into language that students, teachers, coaches, paraprofessionals, other supplemental teachers, and parents can understand. When all the stakeholders share a common understanding, the conversations about student learning will become more focused and meaningful.

Checklists also provide visual and concrete scaffolding that walks students through a process by listing each step in sequential order, asking for responses or examples to make sure they are on track, and allowing them to work at their own pace individually or with a partner to master the task. As author Susan L. Hall (2008) notes:

The teacher may modify the modes of task presentation to help the student understand or increase the structure of the task to make all the steps more explicit. Providing more repetition cycles and more corrective feedback can intensify instruction. (p. 69)

Students require varying types and intensities of scaffolding to be successful. The goal is to gradually remove the scaffolding as the student demonstrates mastery.

Visual Learners

Students live in a world of technology that stimulates their senses through visuals, music, graphics, touch, social interaction, instant communication, and creativity. It is no wonder they sometimes glaze over while reading textbooks or staring at chalkboards. Many of today's students not only want to see more visuals in the classroom, but also *need* these tools to understand what they are learning. Checklists provide a visual framework to scaffold the multistep assignment, helping those students who need visual cues to improve their understanding.

A study by Yale University in 1994 reported that the average U.S. elementary student watched between five and six hours of television a day (Dunn, 1994). Lynell Burmark (2002), author of *Visual Literacy*, discusses how students—including their attention spans—are influenced by the nature of programming. The length of common entertainment forms is getting shorter. Movies used to be two hours, but most are now ninety minutes. Comedy shows are less than thirty minutes, and TV and other media have quick, interwoven visuals, dialogue, and narration.

Students spend their time outside of school immersed in visual, auditory, and kinesthetic stimuli from video games, television, movies, Internet, iPods, iPads, Kindles, and cell phones. Students become used to these highly entertaining forms of communication and feel like they are entering another world when they walk into a traditional classroom with a blackboard, rows of chairs, and ten-pound textbooks piled on bookcases. Burmark (2002) states:

> It's time for teachers to take advantage of the way kids entertain themselves today, to employ those same media and the thinking habits they foster for the betterment of student learning. To do so not only allows another way to reach children, but also stretches us into a greater understanding of how the human mind so wonderfully adapts to and integrates new tools. (p. 3)

Teachers who use more visual imagery in their teaching help students interpret, understand, and appreciate the meaning of visual messages. They also help students communicate more effectively by applying concepts of visual design, producing visual messages, and using visual thinking to conceptualize solutions to problems (Christopherson, 1997). Many teachers are familiar with the concepts of different learning modalities and multiple intelligences (Gardner, 1993), but they may not be as familiar with the physiological basis of these theories.

Author Robert L. Lindstrom (1999) explains the physiological basis of visual thinking by describing how the eyes are the most powerful conduit to the brain because they send information to the cerebral cortex through two optic nerves, each consisting of one million nerve fibers. By comparison, each auditory nerve consists of only thirty thousand fibers. The nerve cells devoted to visual processing account for about 30 percent of the brain's cortex, compared to 8 percent for touch and 3 percent for hearing. Lindstrom says, "With all the bandwidth to the brain, it's no wonder we perceive the world and communicate in visual terms. We read five times as fast as the average person talks. We register a full-color image, the equivalent of a megabyte of data, in a fraction of a second" (as cited in Burmark, 2002, p. 10).

It is no surprise that when Bobby listens to the teacher talk about a response to literature paper, he does not fully understand the concept; only 3 percent of his nerve cells are devoted to hearing. However, if the teacher were to show Bobby a checklist for a response to literature paper, the visual tool would boost his nerve cell activity from 3 percent to 30 percent. If Bobby were to listen to the teacher while looking at the checklist and using a marker to physically check off each section, he could activate 41 percent or more of his nerve cells and become more engaged in his own learning.

Burmark (2002) believes that teachers should become "visually literate" and take advantage of the way kids entertain themselves by using visuals, technology, and media as tools to motivate students to learn. If teachers use more visuals to effectively communicate concepts and solutions to problems, they can help all students learn skills for school and the workplace. The marketplace increasingly draws on visual literacy; "research by 3M corporation shows that people are able to process visual information 60,000 times more quickly than textual information" (Burmark, 2002, p. 5). Newspaper surveys concluded that print material had an average of thirteen seconds to capture the attention of readers, and the most critical hook was visual interest (Burmark, 2002). This extends to other media, too. Television programming strives to hold the attention of the channel surfers, and "Web designers try to create 'sticky' sites where visitors will stay long enough to make purchases online" (Burmark, 2002, p. 5).

If teachers tap into their students' visual intelligence, their students can transfer their visual awareness to schoolwork, increasing their comprehension skills, improving their learning, and keeping their attention so they will want to learn more. Savvy teachers replicate and reinforce the patterns their students learn in their leisure time.

Allan Paivio (1986), author of *Mental Representations*, theorizes that visual and verbal information is encoded and decoded by separate cognitive channels in the brain. He says the visual channel manipulates image elements simultaneously, whereas the linguistic channel functions in a linear, sequential manner. Paivio calls the process by which the same information is presented to the brain in different forms, such as verbal and visual, "dual coding." In which case, the concepts flow seamlessly between their linguistic labels and their visual representations (Burmark, 2002).

Professor Glenda C. Rakes (1999) supports Paivio's theory of dual coding. She reports that medical researchers using positron emission tomography (PET scans) viewed two regions in the brain's verbal domain—the left hemisphere—become active when individuals were asked to listen to and remember verbal information. When the individuals were presented with visual information, the right hemisphere lit up. She concluded that the use of visuals in instructional materials is more than decorative; it provides a dual code that can increase comprehension. Teachers who combine verbal and visual learning experiences target both sides of their students' brains, thereby improving their learning.

A checklist provides a combination of beneficial experiences: it provides written learning experiences because it contains words and questions from the language of the standards; it provides verbal experiences because the teacher talks about the process and students discuss it with each other; and it provides a visual experience because of the lines and boxes that create a flowchart to follow from beginning to end. Everyone learns differently. The more modalities the teacher uses, the greater the number of students who respond positively to the method.

Teachers trained in traditional methodology that relies on lecture, seatwork, textbook quizzes, blackboard work, and multiple-choice tests find it difficult to compete with the fast-paced sound bites and visually and audibly stimulating video games, television shows, movies, and Internet sites students are exposed to constantly. Students born in the 1990s and later have been labeled the iGeneration due to the types of popular digital technologies (iPhone, iPod, iPad, iTunes) (Rosen, 2011). According to a Nielsen company study (Nielsen Wire, 2010), the typical teenager sends and receives 3,339 texts a month and makes or receives 191 phone calls during the same period. Typical teens and preteens switch among use of laptops, cell phones, MP3 players, televisions, and video games with ease at home, but "in school, we require them to unitask by listening to the teacher, completing worksheets, writing with pen and paper, or engaging in other solitary activities. There are better ways of teaching our students" (Rosen, 2011, p. 14).

Marc Prensky (2001), educator and consultant, believes that one of the causes of the decline of education in the United States is that today's students have changed radically. He calls today's students "digital natives" and most educators "digital immigrants" who entered the world of technology later in life. According to Ronald Wolk (2011), author of *Wasting Minds*, "schools must move quickly into the digital age, or they will become increasingly irrelevant to their students and the larger society" (p. 166).

Academic Checklists

Checklists can act as academic to-do lists that delineate the progressions students must complete to be successful. Popham (2008) uses the phrase *progressions of learning* to describe the targeted subskills needed to complete the bigger and more abstract assignment, project, or performance. Students who struggle with a response to literature, for example, need more support than their teacher pointing out that they need to work more on their writing. These students need a road map to help them accomplish the assignment (for example, "create an outline," "write a paragraph," and so on). Teachers also need a road map, one that will help them organize their teaching into logical and meaningful chunks using the language of the standards. They need to be able to pinpoint where students are having trouble and adjust their teaching as needed to focus on those problem areas during the formative assessment period.

Common Assessment Checklist

When teams of teachers collaborate and develop common assessment checklists, all the teachers and all the students are working toward common goals. Figure 6.1 is an example of a common assessment checklist that fourth- and fifth-grade language arts teachers created to help their students write a response to literature paper. This checklist can be given to individual students, used in group work, sent home to parents, or written on chart paper and hung in the classroom. It serves as a visual reminder of what has to be accomplished to meet the state standard of writing an effective response to literature.

Self-assess your response to literature paper using the following questions to guide you. Fill in all the blanks.	Not Yet 0	Yes 1
Did you carefully read the story?		
• What is the main idea? _____		
• What is the major theme? _____		
• What is the author's purpose? _____		
Did you engage the reader at the beginning of your response?		
• Did you start your writing in an interesting way (example: quotation, question, unusual fact)?		
• What is your point of view or perspective? _____		
Did you give a judgment (opinion) about the book?		
• Did you think about your own life as you read and wrote?		
• What are you responding to from the book? _____		
• What opinions do you have about the book? _____		
Did you provide examples to justify your judgment?		
• Did you provide specific examples from the literature?		
• Did you refer to personal examples?		
• Did you refer to other sources (examples: movies, television, other books, experts)?		
Subtotal		

Page 2 Response to Literature Checklist

Criteria/Performance Indicators	Not Yet 0	Yes 1
Did you provide closure to your writing?		
• Do you have a complete summary?		
• Is your summary five or more sentences?		
• Have you restated your topic?		
Did you lift the level of language (descriptive and academic words)?		
• Did you replace at least five words with synonyms? Word: _____ Synonym: _____ Word: _____ Synonym: _____ Word: _____ Synonym: _____ Word: _____ Synonym: _____ Word: _____ Synonym: _____		
• Did you include two figures of speech (idioms, similes, metaphors, hyperboles)? Example 1: _____ Example 2: _____		
• Did you use different transitions (examples: after, first, finally)?		
• Did you include sensory details related to the following? Sight: _____ Sound: _____ Smell: _____ Taste: _____ Touch: _____		
Did you exclude extraneous (unrelated) details from your writing?		
• Did you stay on topic?		
• Did you remove anything that wasn't about your topic?		
Total		

Figure 6.1: Response to literature checklist.

Source: *Created by Sheri Davis, Debra B. Williams, and Pam R. Smith, teachers at Carrollton City Middle School in Carrollton City, Georgia. Used with permission.*

Traditional checklists require a person to simply check off what has been accomplished. This model of a checklist requires students to write out answers as well as check off whether or not they have finished the step. The emphasis on accountability requires students to demonstrate what they know and can do rather than just put a check mark in a box. Sometimes a student may think he or she knows or finished something, but that is not actually the case.

Moreover, teachers need to be able to quickly see if students really know the main idea, theme, and author's purpose for writing the selection. If the majority of the students have a "Not Yet" filled in after the question "What is the major theme?," the teacher may need to reteach the concept of literary theme and give some examples. When the teacher sees that only a small number of students filled in a "Not Yet" for the question "What is your point of view or perspective?," he or she can create a flexible group, provide more targeted instruction about who is telling the story, and give examples of how various authors conveyed point of view in their stories or books. By observing students' responses on their checklists, teachers might discover that they need to reteach the concepts to the whole class, a small group, or an individual student. It is important to clarify any misconceptions early rather than wait until the student turns in the final paper and receives a final grade that cannot be improved.

Struggling students may feel overwhelmed when they see a lengthy checklist, such as the two-page example, delineating what they have to do in order to successfully complete an assignment. One way to differentiate instruction is to give some students just one chunk of the checklist at a time. Students who successfully complete the first chunk and demonstrate their understanding through both oral and written methods will gain confidence. They are then ready to address the second chunk of the process. Other students may want to work independently at their own pace. These students will also gain confidence using the checklist because they feel secure in knowing the requirements.

Students can assess their own work, or students working in teams can assess each other's work using the checklist as a guideline. Parents can help students with the assignment by asking them the questions on the checklist and monitoring their progress. Checklists are usually considered formative assessments and are not graded, but the feedback they provide helps all the stakeholders monitor student progress or lack of progress toward meeting goals.

Problem-Solving Checklist

Another example of a checklist can guide students through complicated multistep problems. Figure 6.2 (pages 69–70) is a problem-solving checklist for middle school students related to understanding transformations in math. The teacher embedded examples and definitions for some of the terms (for example, *polygon* and *vertex*) to help students remember them.

Students are more successful when oral instructions are combined with modeling and written instructions that walk students through each step of the problem-solving process. Teachers can use the visual structure of the checklist to reinforce their verbal instructions by providing examples from another problem, short definitions, and sample answers. In chunking the steps necessary to complete the task, teachers can pinpoint where students become confused and clarify the misunderstanding so they are able to proceed in the process. Students are also more aware of where they need help and can ask specific questions about the problem rather than just raising their hand and saying that they don't understand.

Performance standard—Students will demonstrate understanding of transformations:

a. Demonstrate understanding of translations, dilations, rotations, and reflections, and relate symmetry to appropriate transformations.

b. Given a figure in the coordinate plane, determine the coordinates resulting from a translation, dilation, rotation, or reflection.

Follow the directions within the chart below.	No 0	Yes 1
1. Plot a creative, original polygon (preimage). Did you . . .		
Create an original polygon? Polygon—plane shape having three or more straight sides		
Label the vertices of your original polygon? Vertex—each corner point of the shape Example: A, B, C		
Chart the coordinates of each vertex? Example: (4, -6) (x-coordinate, y-coordinate)		
2. Create a congruent image from the original at (x + 4, y). Did you . . .		
Translate (slide) the original polygon to its new coordinates?		
Label the vertices of your new polygon? Example: A, B, C		
Chart the coordinates of each new vertex?		
3. Create a congruent image from the original at (x, y – 3). Did you . . .		
Translate (slide) the original polygon to its new coordinates?		
Label the vertices of your new polygon?		
Chart the coordinates of each new vertex?		
4. Create a congruent image from the original at (x – 4, y + 1). Did you . . .		
Translate (slide) the original polygon to its new coordinates?		
Label the vertices of your new polygon?		
Chart the coordinates of each new vertex?		

Continued on next page →

5. Provide descriptions of each translations' position, shape, and size. Did you . . .		
Tell what happens to an image when you add units to the original x-coordinates (x + c, y)?		
Tell what happens to an image when you subtract units from the original x-coordinates (x − c, y)?		
Tell what happens to an image when you add units to the original y-coordinates (x, y + c)?		
Tell what happens to an image when you subtract units from the original y-coordinates (x, y − c)?		

Figure 6.2: Coordinating translations checklist.

Source: *Created by Yvonne Stroud, Champion Middle School, DeKalb County, Georgia. Used with permission.*

Behavior Checklists

A number of researchers discuss the "split pyramid" of RTI, which is the RTI pyramid with a vertical split: academic skills on one side and behavioral issues on the other; the same expectations for success rates apply to both sides of the pyramid. In addition to academic monitoring, the RTI framework also includes the monitoring of a student's behavioral patterns to see if they have an impact on his or her academic achievement. Sometimes it becomes apparent that a student's behavior is interfering with his or her learning. Checklists serve as a tool to collect information about a student's behavior; teachers can then analyze the data to try to determine whether or not the behavior could be the cause of the academic problem.

William N. Bender (2009), author of *Beyond the RTI Pyramid*, discusses behavior strategies in the general education classroom:

> General education classes also involve a host of teaching behaviors or actions that are not in the strictest sense "behavioral interventions" since they are not based on a specified behavioral intervention plan and do not result in data collection on any specific behaviors for any specific child. Rather, these behavioral management actions should be considered "good teaching habits" that teachers use to foster positive behaviors in the class. (p. 112)

Such behavior strategies include establishing class rules, setting clear expectations for behavior, supervising transitions between activities, using proximity when a student is off task, and visually monitoring behavior. These strategies could help 80 to 90 percent of the students in Tier 1 behave appropriately.

Tier 2 behavioral interventions target small groups of students or specific students (10 to 15 percent) who have not responded appropriately to the behavior strategies of Tier 1. Tier 2 interventions are more intensive and could include checklists to remind the students of the rules and procedures and to help them self-assess their own study and social skills.

Tier 3 behavioral interventions target the 1 to 5 percent of students who have not responded to the general class or the small-group or individual interventions. Bender (2009) says that "at this level, most researchers recommend conducting a formal functional behavior assessment (FBA) and initiating an individually targeted intervention to assist the student in managing his or her behavior" (p. 115).

According to Maryln Appelbaum (2009), author of *The One-Stop Guide to Implementing RTI*,

> Many behavior problems were actually caused by learning problems. When students cannot learn, they become frustrated. The more frustrated they become, the more likely they are to misbehave. RTI has the potential to revolutionize all this. There will be no more students waiting to fail. (p. xix)

Students' behavior problems need to be addressed so that learning can take place at the highest level possible. Students who struggle with writing in language arts could have additional organizational and behavior problems related to paying attention, following directions, completing tasks on time, cooperating with other students, or remembering to do the work. It may be important to observe the student and look for tools to help the student be successful. If the behavior problem is not addressed, it could lead to a deficit in future learning.

Educators should make an effort to see if the behavior is a learned behavior that can be changed or if it is the result of a disability. Attempting to change a student's behavior is difficult. According to author Martin Henley (2004), direct attempts to change someone's behavior are usually met with resentment and resistance. For many years, teachers and school districts preferred to manage behavior problems with behavior modification techniques that included the use of rewards and punishments. Henley believes that these techniques when used appropriately can be a useful tool, but "the overuse of rewards and punishments places too much emphasis on controlling student behavior and not enough emphasis on teaching students to control their own behavior" (p. 100). Checklists provide students with a chance to take control of their own behavior and monitor themselves rather than relying on tokens or rewards to encourage them to behave appropriately. They become a part of their own assessment. According to researchers Arthur L. Costa and Bena Kallick (1992),

> We must constantly remind ourselves that the ultimate purpose of evaluation is to have students learn to become self-evaluating. If students graduate from our schools still dependent upon others to tell them they are adequate, good, or excellent, then we've missed the whole point of what education is about. (p. 280)

Author Barbara Reider (2005) recommends that teachers provide logical consequences for students who do not follow the rules or procedures so that students see that the consequence is not just punitive. For example, if a student does not work well in a group setting, he or she may have to go to a time-out area and work alone until he or she is ready to demonstrate appropriate cooperative social skills.

Students need social, emotional, and behavioral supports in addition to academic support. Intervention components include the following: classroom management, behavior management, social skills instruction and assessment, self-management skills instruction, understanding of the impact of culture and language on behavior, social-emotional development, functional behavior assessment, and implementation of positive behavioral supports or behavior plans (Hoover, 2009).

Classroom Behavior Checklist

Teachers in Tier 1 usually start with proactive preventive measures at the beginning of the school year geared toward the whole class. Providing clear expectations for behavior on day one and periodically throughout the year as needed sets the tone for the classroom climate. Researcher Robert Marzano (2007) says that the design and implementation of classroom rules and procedures become critical to classroom management. Regardless of how well behaved students in a given class might be, they still need rules and procedures that are established at the beginning of the year and retaught many times throughout the year. Marzano says, "Without effective rules and procedures, teaching (and consequently learning) is inhibited" (p. 117).

Classroom procedures provide the organizational framework for the operational side of teaching. Teachers can follow up their oral instructions with a written checklist to help students learn and remember classroom procedures (Burke, 2008). Figures 6.3, 6.4, and 6.5 (pages 72–74) provide examples of procedural checklists at the elementary and secondary levels. These checklists could be used to set the teaching climate for all students in Tier 1 or along with specific interventions in Tier 2 to help small groups and individual students who have trouble remembering and following classroom procedures.

Self-assess your ability to follow classroom procedures.	No 0	Yes 1
Coming into the classroom: Did you . . .		
Store your backpack or book bag?		
Walk in quietly before the bell rang?		
Take your assigned seat?		
Books, supplies, and homework: Did you . . .		
Bring your books to class?		
Bring paper, a pencil, and a pen?		
Bring your completed homework?		
Whole-class activities: Did you . . .		
Pay attention to the teacher?		

Raise your hand to ask a question?		
Listen to the teacher and other students?		
Small-group activities: Did you . . .		
Form your group quickly and quietly?		
Follow your role assignment?		
Respect the opinions of others?		
Leaving class: Did you . . .		
Put away your work and supplies?		
Write your homework in your notebook?		
Help clean up the room?		

Figure 6.3: Procedure checklist for elementary students.

Self-assess your ability to follow classroom procedures.	No 0	Yes 1
Arrival and Departure		
Were you in your seat before the bell rang?		
Did you bring what you needed from your locker?		
Did you wait for the teacher to dismiss you at the end of the period?		
Preparation		
Did you have your textbook?		
Did you have your supplies?		
Did you have any paperwork (tardy slips, absentee slips, admittance slips)?		
Homework and Makeup Work		
Did you bring your finished homework?		
Did you write down new homework assignments?		
Did you turn in all makeup work within one day of being absent?		
Group Work		
Did you move quietly and quickly into your assigned group?		
Did you follow your role assignment?		
Did you cooperate with your group members?		

Continued on next page →

Interruptions		
Did you listen to all intercom announcements?		
Did you turn off all electronic devices?		
Did you respect your teacher and other students by not interrupting them when they spoke?		

Figure 6.4: Procedure checklist for secondary students.

Self-assess your ability to follow all classroom behavior expectations.	No 0	Yes 1
School and classroom rules: Did you . . .		
Obey all school rules?		
Follow all classroom expectations?		
Contribute positively to the classroom climate?		
Respect: Did you . . .		
Respect the ideas, opinions, and customs of others?		
Respect the classroom environment?		
Respect other people's property?		
Participation: Did you . . .		
Participate in the classroom community?		
Participate in the school community?		
Participate in your own learning?		
Quality work: Did you . . .		
Strive for excellence?		
Take pride in your work and ideas?		
Value learning and academic achievement?		
Social skills: Did you . . .		
Listen to others?		
Empathize with the feelings of others?		
Cooperate with others?		

Figure 6.5: Classroom behavior expectation checklist.

Group-Work Checklist

A student who is struggling academically may have difficulty working with peers in groups to complete assignments or projects. Teachers can use visual tools to help focus these students. For example, figure 6.6 is an example of a group-work checklist that may help individual students within a group work well together and self-assess their efforts.

Self-assess your ability to work well in a group by answering the following questions.	No 0	Yes 1
Cooperation: Did you . . .		
Follow your role assignment?		
Take turns when talking?		
Contribute to the group?		
Respect others?		
Communication: Did you . . .		
Ask good questions?		
Speak clearly and loudly enough to be heard?		
Listen to others without interrupting?		
Respond appropriately to comments?		
Encouragement: Did you . . .		
Check for understanding?		
Provide positive verbal feedback (kind words)?		
Provide positive nonverbal feedback (gestures, facial expressions, eye contact)?		
Problem solving: Did you . . .		
Disagree with the idea, not the person?		
Consider multiple options?		
Brainstorm possible solutions?		
Arrive at a consensus through negotiation?		

Figure 6.6: Student group-work checklist.

Individual Student Behavior Checklist

A Tier 2 or 3 intervention could include a behavior checklist designed for a student who has special behavior problems that may not be covered in the whole-class or group-work checklists.

Teachers can create a personalized checklist for an individual student that targets his or her problem areas. Figure 6.7 is an example of such a checklist. Checklists help students self-assess their actions and reflect on how they can improve their behavior, organization, social skills, and study skills. This helps students improve not only their academic achievement, but also their interpersonal skills.

Self-assess your organization skills and behavior by answering the following questions.	No 0	Yes 1
Self-discipline: Did you . . .		
Listen attentively in class?		
Complete your work?		
Focus on the task?		
Organization: Did you . . .		
Bring supplies to class?		
Bring all assigned work?		
Write down homework assignments?		
Social skills: Did you . . .		
Respect the space of others?		
Listen attentively to others?		
Cooperate with others?		
Quality work: Did you . . .		
Check your work more than once?		
Ask for help when needed?		
Take pride in your work?		
Study skills: Did you . . .		
Take good notes in class?		
Create study sheets for tests?		
Complete all homework assignments?		

Figure 6.7: Individual student behavior checklist.

Functional Behavior Assessment

In addition to having students self-assess their behavior and work habits, the teacher and other interventionists at Tier 2 or Tier 3 may need to observe a student's behaviors to determine the type of misbehavior, what caused the student to misbehave, and what happened after the behavior occurred. The functional behavior assessment (FBA) involves the systematic collection of data and information about a student's behavior and the antecedents that cause it and the consequences that result from it (Shores, 2009). According to Cara Shores (2009), author of *A Comprehensive RTI Model,*

> FBA is instrumental in planning interventions for all students with behavioral problems and may be used with children who are unresponsive to tier 1 universal interventions. It is most commonly used with tier 2 nonresponders. It is required for students with emotional behavioral disorders and is sometimes an integral part of evaluation for other areas of special education eligibility. (p. 17)

The FBA process tries to determine why a disruptive behavior is occurring. The ABC strategy is part of the FBA process; it provides a graphic chart similar to a checklist to record observable data: *A* stands for the antecedent, or the event that occurs before the behavior; *B* stands for the behavior; and *C* stands for the consequence. Appelbaum (2009) says that one has to "look at what was occurring prior to the behavior, look at the behavior, and then look at what occurs as a result of the behavior" (p. 89). Sometimes students may misbehave and the antecedent is not obvious. For example, Teddy throws down his book and storms out of the classroom. He may be reacting to an academic task that was too hard or a change in his schedule that disrupted his routine. He may be tired from staying up late the night before or hungry because he missed breakfast. Bender (2009) says that "once the function of the behavior has been determined, teachers can usually identify the antecedents that will result in more acceptable behaviors. Teachers then develop an intervention to provide those desired behavioral consequences" (p. 115).

Figure 6.8 shows a sample ABC observation chart used to chronicle incidents impartially over several sessions to discover a pattern. This assists in determining the next steps (Appelbaum, 2009).

Date	Antecedent	Behavior	Consequence	Observer

Figure 6.8: ABC chart for observed behaviors.

In Conclusion

Gawande (2010) wrote about the importance of the checklist to help adults manage all the knowledge and complexities of the 21st century and reduce the number of mistakes made. If surgeons, scientists, and other such well-educated professionals need checklists to help guide them in their jobs and maintain quality, doesn't it seem likely that struggling middle school students would also need some guidance when they are writing a response to literature about a text they barely understand? Teachers are visual learners, too, and checklists make it easier to record and analyze data related to students' academic and behavior patterns that impact achievement and socialization. Checklists provide both support for the struggling student and the structure to allow students who have mastered the material to work independently at their own pace. Checklists help ensure that each student in the class feels he or she has the opportunity to participate in class activities and contribute to the classroom community. Furthermore, they provide students with the framework for becoming successful adults who can meet the challenges of the 21st century by managing and organizing their own knowledge and skills successfully.

Chapter 7

Rubrics as an Assessment Tool

A rubric is a tool that provides students with a clear picture of desired results. The purpose of a rubric is to define the criteria and highlight the standards and elements of a task that are necessary to complete the assignment with a high level of success. Teachers use rubrics to help guide students to the desired outcome. Rubrics are also useful in helping parents understand the current level of student performance.

Rubrics are an assessment tool; the criteria create a formative path for students to follow during their demonstrations of understanding. Teachers are able to evaluate a student's current level of performance, and the rubric descriptors highlight the next levels of expected performance. As a result, a rubric is not only an assessment tool, it provides feedback as well.

Analytical Rubrics

Analytical rubrics provide a formative approach to the analysis of student performance. This type of rubric includes detailed descriptors of quality and multiple levels of student performance. Figure 7.1 (page 80) is an example of an analytical rubric for a writing activity that could be used in grades 4 and up. It is a four-point rubric, as indicated by the points listed across the top row of the rubric. The criteria listed in the first column are those deemed necessary for the successful completion of the task. Descriptors of quality are written at the intersection of each criterion and point value.

Writing Rubric	1 Point	2 Points	3 Points	4 Points
Idea Development	Topic is unclear.	Writer strays from topic.	Topic is focused.	Examples and details bring the topic to life.
	Key ideas do not exist or are difficult to identify.	Additional key ideas or details are needed.	Key ideas and details are clearly expressed.	Clearly expressed details and key ideas enhance the theme or story line.
Organization	Composition lacks structure.	Composition is loosely structured.	Composition is appropriately structured or formatted.	Structure assists in supporting the story.
	Composition lacks logical order.	Order is scattered, difficult to follow.	Order is logical.	Order is logical and effective.
	Introduction and conclusion are weak.	Introduction or conclusion is weak.	Introduction and conclusion are effective.	Introduction is strong, and conclusion is satisfying.
	Composition lacks topic sentences.	Attempt was made to incorporate topic sentences.	Composition has clear topic sentences.	Composition has effective topic sentences.
	Composition lacks transitions.	Some transitions are used.	Transitions are used appropriately.	Transitions within and between paragraphs create a smooth flow.
Word Choice	Word choice is vague and confusing.	Word choice is limited or simplistic.	Word choice is clear and functional.	Word choice is precise, detailed, and interesting.
Voice	Connection to the audience is missing.	Voice is present but not appropriate for purpose.	Voice fits topic, purpose, and audience.	Voice fits topic, purpose, and audience; writer's personality is apparent.
Fluency	Composition has simple, monotonous sentences.	Composition has mostly simple sentences.	Composition has mostly varied sentences.	Sentences vary in structure and length.
	Fragments and run-ons prevent understanding.	Fragments and run-ons interfere with understanding.	There are few fragments or run-ons, and they do not interfere with understanding.	Composition has well-crafted sentences.
Conventions	Errors interfere with the reader's ability to understand.	Errors are distracting but do not interfere with understanding.	Errors are infrequent and do not interfere with understanding.	Errors are unnoticeable.
Total points earned:				

Figure 7.1: Analytical rubric for writing assignment.

Rubrics should be given to students prior to completing their work. The rubric's descriptors guide students to high levels of quality because the expectations are clear, written, and available throughout the completion of the task. Examples of previously completed assignments are helpful when first introducing the rubric to students to ensure understanding.

When evaluating with the rubric, the teacher provides feedback by highlighting which point value the student has earned for the criterion listed. Although the rubric shown in figure 7.1 is divided into the six areas of writing, the student is being judged and being provided with feedback on twelve aspects of the writing process as indicated by each rubric row.

Holistic Rubrics

Holistic rubrics are written in a different format than are analytical rubrics. Teachers should include criteria important to the successful completion of the task, just as with the analytical rubric. However, in a holistic rubric, teachers group criteria under single point values. Holistic rubrics are designed with a parallel construction; all descriptors for the point value are listed underneath that specific value, and the first line of every point value deals with the same focus or topic, as does the second line, the third line, and so on. Students receive a single score for their completed work.

The holistic rubric is more summative in nature; students don't receive the same level of formative feedback as they do with an analytical rubric. The holistic rubric reflects a student's overall performance, whereas an analytical rubric gives the exact descriptor that fits each aspect of a performance. Figure 7.2 (pages 82–83) shows the point and criterion system used in a holistic rubric, illustrating the exact same information as the writing rubric shown in figure 7.1; the only difference is the format used.

Giving a score based on a holistic rubric requires choosing one point value for the entire piece of work. However, a student's work rarely meets every criterion within the same point value. As a result, the point value is only accurate for some of the descriptors.

Gathering data is important when evaluating students with RTI in mind. The holistic rubric does not provide the detailed information needed to track the success rate of the student on all aspects of the product, performance, or behavior. Although the holistic rubric has its place in evaluating student work, the analytical rubric provides the best fit for evaluating students within the RTI framework.

4 Points

Examples and details bring the topic to life.

Clearly expressed details and key ideas enhance the theme or story line.

Structure assists in supporting the story.

Order is logical and effective.

Introduction is strong, and conclusion is satisfying.

Composition has effective topic sentences.

Transitions within and between paragraphs create a smooth flow.

Word choice is precise, detailed, and interesting.

Tone fits topic, purpose, and audience; writer's personality is apparent.

Sentences are varied in structure and length.

Composition has well-crafted sentences.

Errors are unnoticeable.

3 Points

Topic is focused.

Key ideas and details are clearly expressed.

Composition is appropriately structured or formatted.

Order is logical.

Introduction and conclusion are effective.

Composition has clear topic sentences.

Transitions are used appropriately.

Word choice is clear and functional.

Tone fits topic, purpose, and audience.

Composition has mostly varied sentences.

There are few fragments or run-ons, and they do not interfere with understanding.

Errors are infrequent and do not interfere with understanding.

2 Points

Writer strays from topic.

Additional key ideas or details are needed.

Composition is loosely structured.

Order is scattered, difficult to follow.

Introduction or conclusion is weak.

Attempt was made to incorporate topic sentences.

Some transitions are used.

Word choice is limited or simplistic.

Tone is present but not appropriate for purpose.

Composition has mostly simple sentences.

Fragments and run-ons interfere with understanding.

Errors are distracting but do not interfere with understanding.

I Point
Topic is unclear.
Key ideas do not exist or are difficult to identify.
Composition lacks structure.
Composition lacks logical order.
Introduction and conclusion are weak.
Composition lacks topic sentences.
Composition lacks transitions.
Word choice is vague and confusing.
Connection to the audience is missing.
Composition has simple, monotonous sentences.
Fragments and run-ons prevent understanding.
Errors interfere with the reader's ability to understand.

Figure 7.2: Holistic rubric for writing assignment.

Designing a Rubric

The remainder of this chapter will focus on the analytical rubric because of its ability to provide students with the feedback they need to improve their performance. Helping students succeed at Tier 1 will lead to fewer students in need of interventions in Tiers 2 and 3. Students already involved in interventions will find the feedback useful as well because it helps them understand their current performance and provides a map leading to the next levels of success.

There are four basic steps to rubric design:

1. Select a scale.

2. Determine the order of point values.

3. Determine the success criteria.

4. Write descriptors.

Select a Scale

Teachers should select a rubric scale that best meets the needs of the project, performance, standard, subject, or behavior being evaluated. Four-point scales are frequently used and can accommodate most purposes. Often scales reflect performance practices within a district or state or province. For example, if a four-point scale is used, the scale might relate to descriptors such as *beginning, developing, proficient,* and *beyond proficient.* Corresponding numerical values are necessary so that data are tracked and compared to other data collected in the grade level, school, or district.

Scales typically start with one rather than zero. Descriptors with a value of zero would include "no evidence of the understanding," "not apparent," "not included," or other similar statements. Ideally, all students will produce some evidence of understanding. If there is no evidence of the criterion, a student can receive a zero even though no descriptors are written for that point value. Students should know in advance that they are expected to demonstrate some level of performance for all criteria, and if this doesn't happen, a zero is the result. Since a zero is unacceptable, students will still need to provide evidence they possess the required skill in a future evaluation.

When selecting the number of points to be used, keep the descriptors in mind. If the point values are too broad, writing descriptors will be difficult. If there is no apparent difference between a descriptor worth five points and a descriptor worth six, perhaps there are too many values for the criterion. Match the complexity of the task to be evaluated by the rubric with the number of points required to clearly define the various levels of quality. If it is clear that more than four points are required due to the extensive nature of the descriptors, a five- or six-point rubric might be in order.

Also keep in mind the age of the students using the rubric. The goal is for the rubric to provide helpful feedback that can lead students to the next level of performance. Therefore, you should choose point values that will allow for quality, meaningful descriptors. Increased point values add to the complexity of both writing and interpreting the rubrics.

Determine the Order of Point Values

The creator of the rubric must also decide the order for listing the point values. The rubric can begin with the highest point value on the left, or it can begin with the lowest on the left and proceed to the highest on the right. The rubrics used as examples in this chapter begin with the lowest number on the left (for example, fig. 7.3). Students read from left to right; therefore, the rubric is designed following this format. The quality and intensity of performance also increase from left to right; therefore, the level of sophistication builds as the rubric descriptors unfold.

Criteria	1	2	3	4

Figure 7.3: Order of point values: lowest to highest.

This is not to say that the opposite point value order is incorrect. Often rubrics that begin with the highest point value on the left are designed to do so to guarantee that students are well aware of the highest expectations in each category. If teachers expect students to reach high levels of performance, it is natural to want to place emphasis on that level through the design of the rubric. However, when rubrics are used formatively, it is helpful for students to understand process steps in a procedure or performance. In this case, left-to-right, lowest-to-highest placement is the better choice.

Determine the Success Criteria

Teachers should select criteria based on their direct relationship to the successful completion of the project, performance, or attainment of a standard. The rubric needs to include all of the criteria associated with a quality outcome. Determining the evaluative criteria is the most important task during rubric creation (Popham, 2002).

The rubric criteria inform the student of the important components of the task. Keep in mind the age of the students. When working with young students, it is better to have two shorter rubrics than one of great length. The rubric is meant to assist the student; it should not be overwhelming or confusing. Three to ten criteria are typical. Early elementary may have one to four criteria. Upper elementary would be likely to have four to six criteria. Middle schools and high schools would likely have ranges from six to ten criteria.

Write Descriptors

Clearly written descriptors are the key to an effective rubric. Descriptors should be designed to help students understand their current performance and to assist them in analyzing the steps necessary to achieve a higher level of success. Students need to fully understand the descriptors. Kid-friendly language results in a deeper understanding of the content within the rubric. If the descriptors make sense to the students, they'll be more likely to use the rubric and learn from it.

Well-written descriptors state performance expectations. As much as possible, state what is expected, not what is *not* desired in the performance. In other words, rather than telling students what not to do, let them know what quality looks like. For example, instead of "Sentences don't usually start with the same word," write "Sentences begin with a wide variety of words." When introducing a new rubric, time should be spent explaining the descriptors to the students. Examples at various performance levels can increase student understanding of expectations.

It is tempting to use numbers within descriptors. When evaluating conventions, descriptors like those listed in figure 7.4 are often used. Numbers provide quantity but do not address quality.

	1	2	3	4
Conventions	9 or more errors	6–8 errors	3–5 errors	0–2 errors

Figure 7.4: Conventions portion of a writing rubric, example 1.

Figure 7.5 (page 86) is a quality alternative. As students become proficient writers, the length of their work grows. Counting errors can be tedious and labor intensive for the teacher. It is also an unnecessary task. It is more important to let students know the impact that those errors have on the reader, in turn making it the student's responsibility to locate and correct them.

	1	2	3	4
Conventions	Errors are so frequent that writing cannot be understood.	Errors are frequent, yet writing can be understood with difficulty.	Errors are infrequent but interfere with the flow of the writing.	Errors are nonexistent or unnoticeable.

Figure 7.5: Conventions portion of a writing rubric, example 2.

When writing rubrics, a verb list is a helpful tool. Coming up with just the right word can be difficult. Choosing from a list saves time and often provides the perfect word for the occasion. Teachers can also quickly identify age-appropriate vocabulary when a list provides a variety of choices. Searching "verb list" online produces many possibilities.

Types of Analytical Rubrics

Rubrics can be designed to meet a variety of purposes. Standards-based, building-block, weighted, and behavior rubrics, each with a different purpose, all still serve to analyze current student performance, track student progress, and compare results to that of peers.

Standards-Based Rubrics

In a standards-based rubric, teachers use national, state or provincial, or local standards as the criteria important to the successful completion of the task. Standards are placed in the first column of the rubric. Lengthy standards need to be dissected into the criteria listed within the standard, each listed separately. For example, if the standard states that students will use pictures, diagrams, and text to describe characters, settings, and events, the rubric should address these criteria separately, as illustrated in figure 7.6. Use the language embedded in the standard when developing the criteria.

	1	2	3	4
Characterization	Student can name the characters in the story.	Student can describe some characters using pictures, diagrams, **or** text.	Student can describe characters using pictures, diagrams, **or** text.	Student can describe characters using a combination of pictures, diagrams, **and** text.
Setting	Student is aware of the setting of the story.	Student can describe some aspects of the setting using pictures, diagrams, **or** text.	Student can describe the setting using pictures, diagrams, **or** text.	Student can describe the setting using a combination of pictures, diagrams, **and** text.
Events	Student can name some key events in the story.	Student can describe some key events using pictures, diagrams, **or** text.	Student can describe key events using pictures, diagrams, **or** text.	Student can describe all key events using a combination of pictures, diagrams, **and** text.

Figure 7.6: Standards-based rubric for reading: characterization, setting, and events.

The teacher should determine the values according to those typically used in the state or province, district, or school. Value labels like *minimal, basic, proficient,* and *advanced* could be used in place of numerical values. Pictures showing progressing levels of success could also be employed, as illustrated in figure 7.7. Regardless of the label used, a point value should be associated with the data so that they can be compared and tracked.

Figure 7.7 is an example of another standards-based rubric. Kindergarten numeracy math standards were used to build this tool. Each standard in the left column has corresponding descriptors for each level of proficiency highlighted in the rubric.

	☺	☺ ☺	☺ ☺ ☺	☺ ☺ ☺ ☺
Counts to 100	Student counts to less than 50.	Student counts to 100 with some prompting.	Student counts to 100 with no prompting.	Student can count beyond 100.
Counts by 10s	Student cannot count by 10s.	Student counts by 10s with inconsistent accuracy.	Student can count by 10s consistently to 100.	Student can count by 10s consistently beyond 100.
Sequences Numbers	Student has difficulty counting forward or backward starting at numbers other than 1 or 100.	Student can count either forward or backward starting at various numbers between 1 and 100 with some prompting.	Student can count forward and backward from numbers between 1 and 100 with some prompting.	Student can count forward and backward from numbers between 1 and 100 independently.
Writes Numbers	Student needs assistance to write numbers.	Student can accurately write most numbers.	Student can accurately write the numbers 1–20 with minimal assistance.	Student can consistently and accurately write the numbers 1–20 independently.

Figure 7.7: Kindergarten rubric for numbers.

Such rubrics can be used multiple times to evaluate student progress and to compare one student to another. When the teacher is confident that the student has reached proficiency, the student no longer needs to be evaluated on that component of the rubric.

Tracking data is important to ensuring that the student's needs are being met. Figure 7.8 (page 88) illustrates one method for tracking rubric data. Teachers should keep records over time so student growth can be monitored and comparisons can be made—two comparisons in particular, both of which are important to the RTI framework. First, the student's work can be compared to that of others in the class to see if he or she is making progress similar to his or her peers. Second, the student's work can be compared to his or her past work to see if he or she is making personal progress. Both comparisons will help a teacher determine what, if any, intervention is needed for the student.

Color coding data is helpful. For example, in figure 7.8 (page 88), the shading helps the teacher spot the difficulties Evan is having. It becomes apparent that he has not reached proficiency in any

	Counts to 100					Counts by 10s					Sequences numbers					Writes numbers				
	Assessment 1	Assessment 2	Assessment 3	Assessment 4	Met Proficiency	Assessment 1	Assessment 2	Assessment 3	Assessment 4	Met Proficiency	Assessment 1	Assessment 2	Assessment 3	Assessment 4	Met Proficiency	Assessment 1	Assessment 2	Assessment 3	Assessment 4	Met Proficiency
Dale	1	2	3	4	Yes	2	2	2	4	Yes	1	2	3	4	Yes	1	2	3	4	Yes
Elissa	2	2	3	4	Yes	2	2	2	4	Yes	1	2	3	4	Yes	1	2	3	4	Yes
Ellen	2	2	3	4	Yes	2	3	3	4	Yes	1	2	3	3	No	2	2	3	4	Yes
Evan	2	2	2	2	No	2	3	3		No	1	2	2	3	No	1	2	3	3	No
James	3	3	4		Yes	3	3	4		Yes	1	2	2	3	No	1	2	2	2	No
Jordan	2	3	4		Yes	3	3	4		Yes	1	2	3	3	No	2	2	2	2	No
Juan	2	3	4		Yes	3	3	4		Yes	1	2	3	4	Yes	1	2	3	4	Yes
Latoya	2	3	4		Yes	3	3	4		Yes	2	2	3	4	Yes	2	2	3	4	Yes
Maria	1	2	4	4	Yes	2	2	3	4	Yes	2	2	3	4	Yes	2	2	3	4	Yes
Meghan	1	2	3	4	Yes	2	2	4		Yes	1	2	3	4	Yes	1	2	2	4	Yes
Natalie	1	2	3	4	Yes	2	3	4		Yes	1	2	3	4	Yes	1	2	3	4	Yes
Nate	1	2	3	4	Yes	2	1	2	4	Yes	1	2	4		Yes	1	2	2	4	Yes
Regina	2	3	4		Yes	3	1	2	4	Yes	1	2	3	4	Yes	1	1	2	4	Yes

Figure 7.8: Data associated with kindergarten rubric for numbers.

of the four areas tested and may require additional time in an intervention to help eliminate the gap he is currently experiencing.

Building-Block Rubrics

Building-block rubrics got their name because of the design. The building-block nature of the rubric centers on the descriptors used within the rubric. Figure 7.9 illustrates the design style. The first point value indicates the first step for the student. In this case, the student can recognize the lower- or uppercase letter. The second point value builds on the first; the student can now recognize both the upper- and lowercase letters. The words *and* and *or* are helpful when writing descriptors as they lead to a logical progression of understanding. For three points, the student has to show that he or she can complete level two and can also print the letters. To earn four points, the student must also say a word that begins with the letter.

In a building-block rubric, the progression is written in order of sophistication. In order to get a three, the student must be able to show that he or she can earn a two. In order to earn a four, the student must be able to earn a three. The design makes the next step to a higher level of expertise very clear to the student. This particular rubric can be used repeatedly to analyze a student's knowledge of each letter of the alphabet independently.

	1	2	3	4
Letter Recognition	Student can: • recognize the lower- or uppercase letter	Student can: • recognize the lower- and uppercase letters	Student can: • recognize the lower- and uppercase letters • print the lower- and uppercase letters	Student can: • recognize the lower- and uppercase letters • print the lower- and uppercase letters • say a word that begins with the letter

Figure 7.9: Rubric for early elementary letter recognition.

Weighted Rubrics

Any rubric, regardless of the design, can also have a component that weights the impact of a rubric category, emphasizing the importance of some more than others. This is beneficial when the rubric is related to a task or specific product for which some criteria are more significant than others. Of course, all criteria need to be on the rubric to help lead students to the desired end, yet some may have increased importance when considering standards and the crucial nature of each.

Figure 7.10 (page 90) provides an example of a weighted rubric, which also displays the building-block method of writing descriptors. The intent of this rubric is to help elementary school students understand the components of a graph. Although it is important for students to include all parts of the graph, this rubric emphasizes the accuracy of the graphed information. Weighting is helpful when using the rubric to determine a grade, but ultimately, the student needs to demonstrate competency with all of the criteria. However, if a student is unable to perform adequately in an area that is weighted, the response may be more immediate and intensive than if the category is deemed less important. For example, in figure 7.10, if a student cannot graph accurately, it is important to intervene. Graphing is a skill that is needed across content areas. If the student has difficulty spelling the title correctly, however, the issue can be dealt with the next time the student needs to create a graph, because it doesn't interfere with the knowledge or performance of the graphing standard. Spelling is also dealt with in a variety of other venues and is not essential to understanding graphing procedures.

	1	2	3	4	Weight
Title of graph	Present	• Present • Does not relate to graph contents	• Present • Relates to content	• Present • Relates to content • No mechanical errors	x 1 = _____
Titles on axes	Present	• Present • Do not relate to graph contents	• Present • Relate to content	• Present • Relate to content • No mechanical errors	x 1 = _____
Numbering/ labeling of x-axis	Inaccurate	• Present • Minor error	• Present • Error free	• Present • Error free • Perfect positioning	x 1 = _____
Numbering/ labeling of y-axis	Inaccurate	• Present • Minor error	• Present • Error free	• Present • Error free • Perfect positioning	x 1 = _____
Accuracy of graphing	Mostly incomplete or inaccurate	• Complete • Minor inaccuracy	• Complete • Accurate	• Complete • Accurate • Well organized, easy to read	x 4 = _____

Figure 7.10: Rubric for a graph analysis.

Weight can also be added to different criteria at different times. For example, when teaching the various components of the writing process, an emphasis will cause the student to pay increased attention to a specific criterion as his or her skills grow. With one piece of writing, the teacher could add a weight to word choice, and with the next piece, she could stress organization. In time, a weight appropriate to the entire writing process can be established to balance the criterion as related to its level of priority in a finished product.

Behavior Rubrics

Creating a behavior rubric requires the same process as an academic rubric, both in design and data collection. These rubrics can be created for an individual student, or they can be designed more generically to cover areas that are most often linked to problem behaviors. Behavior rubrics should concentrate on the few criteria linked to the behavior in greatest need of change. The descriptors are not intended to give students ideas on poor behavior or performance, but instead to help them understand the path to success by providing direction on how to meet expectations.

Figure 7.11 provides an example of a rubric intended to be used with a student who has difficulty producing homework. Initially, the teacher and student would have a conversation about homework completion. Reasons for incompletion would be addressed so it is clear that there are not major roadblocks preventing the student from finishing the work. At that point, they would identify the criteria and write the descriptors to help the student self-evaluate on a daily basis. The teacher evaluates the student daily as well, using the same rubric. Tracking the data will show progress, which should be shared with the student and parents. The rubric will also identify any area that is more problematic than others. The rubric continues to be used until the student develops a positive habit in this area.

	1	2	3
Location	At home	In school	In classroom
Timeliness	More than three days late	One to two days late	On time
Completion	Not started	Not finished	Completed
Quality	Poor quality	Shows some effort	Well done

Figure 7.11: Homework completion rubric.

Rubrics addressing only the expected behavior can also be used. These rubrics are similar to a checklist, but there is one descriptor of quality stating the expected behavior for each criterion. The difference between a rubric of quality and a checklist is that a checklist may list the criteria without any descriptors of quality. As a result, the student knows the criteria but does not necessarily know what proficiency looks like. A rubric of quality lists and clarifies the expectation. The benefit is that the rubric doesn't display unwanted behaviors. An example of this type of rubric is shown in figure 7.12 (page 92).

		Yes	No
Language	Used appropriate language throughout the class period		
Respect	Treated classmates with respect		
Physicality	Kept hands and objects to self		
Collaboration	Worked collaboratively with others in the class		
Contributions	Contributed positively to class discussions		
Daily Total			

Figure 7.12: Rubric for classroom behavior.

The goal of behavior rubrics is to improve student behavior. Students can provide valuable input for rubric criteria and descriptors. Such input may lead to increased ownership and a more successful outcome. The rubrics can also be used to track the performance of individual students and provide valuable data for next steps should the student's behavior indicate that a Tier 2 or 3 intervention is needed.

Scoring Rubrics

To obtain meaningful data, accurate scoring is crucial. Rubric scoring is a matching game; the project, performance, or behavior is matched with the most appropriate descriptor. Although hard work is appreciated, the teacher evaluates only the output so that feedback matches the performance and accurate information is provided to the student. Through this process, the student gains a good understanding of where he or she is and what needs to be accomplished to improve.

A well-written rubric will promote inter-rater reliability; multiple scorers using the same rubric should get the same results when scoring the same product. Likewise, well-written descriptors and the matching process promote reliability. Reliable and comparable results are needed to evaluate student progress and could lead to increased levels of academic or behavioral support through the RTI process. When the same rubric is used by more than one teacher, initially scoring together and discussing the results will increase the likelihood that scoring practices will be dependable.

Highlight the descriptors that best match student performance to score a rubric. If a total score is desired, add the values associated with the highlighted areas to produce the total score. A total score gives limited information, although it may be appropriate for summative evaluation. For a formative evaluation, additional information is required. Tracking the data by criterion is important because it gives the clearest picture of how students are currently performing and what they need to do to get to the next level.

Figure 7.13 provides an example of a rubric used to evaluate performance in a physical education class. This rubric is marked to show one way that scoring can be accomplished.

Another scoring method requires less paper, less time, one rubric, and a gradebook. Place students' scores immediately into the gradebook when scoring takes place, thereby eliminating the step of marking the rubric then transferring the rubric results into a gradebook. Because students do need to understand how they scored, this method works well with electronic gradebooks when students have online access to their scores. Because students have a copy of the rubric, they can compare their scores in the gradebook with the descriptors on the rubric to better understand their performance.

	1	2	3	4
Warm-ups	Activity is not done as assigned. Effort is poor, and/or heart rate does not increase. X	Activity is done as assigned, but student shows inconsistent effort. Heart rate increases only slightly.	Activity is done as assigned. Heart rate increases but not to appropriate extent.	Activity is done as assigned with continuous movement. Heart rate increases to appropriate extent.
Stretches	Body position is incorrect. Student shows no effort. Student shows no improvement.	Body position is partially correct. Student shows little to no effort. Student shows little or no improvement. X	Body position is correct. Student shows some effort. Student shows improvement.	Body position is correct. Student shows maximum effort. Student shows improvement.
On Task	Student does not listen to presentation. Student is not willing to follow directions.	Student listens to presentation. Student follows directions some of the time. Student is off task and makes questionable decisions. X	Student listens to presentation. Student follows directions most of the time. Student stays on task most of the time and makes good decisions.	Student listens to presentation. Student follows directions accurately. Student stays on task and makes good decisions.
Total = 5 of a possible 12				

Figure 7.13: Rubric for physical education performance.

When Grading Is Necessary

When a formative assessment is used, grading is not recommended. A grade is intended to reflect what students know and can do after instruction and appropriate practice. A formative assessment is intended to give feedback for improvement so that the teacher and student can take appropriate actions to display a higher level of performance. Its purpose is not to obtain a grade (O'Connor, 2009). Until there is an expectation that students should be able to perform a skill and demonstrate their understanding of a practice, grades should be avoided. After ample opportunity is given for practice, however, the assessment becomes summative, and a grade may be required. Teachers can use the same rubric for both formative and summative assessments.

If the grade is to accurately reflect student performance, careful consideration is necessary when turning the rubric score into a grade. Usually, there are five grades to choose from: A, B, C, D, and F. A rubric usually has four categories, and for that reason, the typical conversion will not work. In the case of a typical percent, the score earned would be divided by the points possible. Scoring a four-point rubric by percent would produce a low score not reflective of the performance. For example, if a student earns all threes on a four-point rubric, the percentage score would be 75 percent. The problem is that 75 percent is often a C or a D grade, yet a three on a rubric shows competence.

Consider the solutions shown in figures 7.14 and 7.15 when a grade is required. Using these methods will result in a grade that more accurately reflects student performance.

Steps	Illustration					Grading Key
Count the number of criteria.	Rubric	1	2	3	4	above 3.2 to 4.0 = A
	Criteria 1			x		above 2.4 to 3.2 = B
	Criteria 2		x			above 1.6 to 2.4 = C
	Criteria 3				x	above 0.8 to 1.6 = D
	Criteria 4				x	0 to 0.8 = F
	Criteria 5			x		
	Criteria 6			x		
	Criteria 7				x	
	Criteria 8			x		
Determine the number of points earned.	8 criteria, 26 points earned (out of 32)					
Divide the points earned by number of criteria.	26 / 8 = 3.25					
Use the grading key to determine the grade.	Grade = A					

Figure 7.14: Changing a rubric score to a grade, solution 1.

If using these solutions, adjust the spans to meet the grading needs within your school. Of course, you can also develop other solutions for turning the points available on the four-point rubric into a five-point grading scale. These are just examples.

Steps	Illustration	Grading Key
Count the number of criteria. The lowest grade ranges from zero to the number of criteria.	<table><tr><td>Rubric</td><td>1</td><td>2</td><td>3</td><td>4</td></tr><tr><td>Criteria 1</td><td></td><td></td><td>x</td><td></td></tr><tr><td>Criteria 2</td><td></td><td>x</td><td></td><td></td></tr><tr><td>Criteria 3</td><td></td><td></td><td></td><td>x</td></tr><tr><td>Criteria 4</td><td></td><td></td><td></td><td>x</td></tr><tr><td>Criteria 5</td><td></td><td></td><td>x</td><td></td></tr><tr><td>Criteria 6</td><td></td><td></td><td>x</td><td></td></tr><tr><td>Criteria 7</td><td></td><td></td><td></td><td>x</td></tr><tr><td>Criteria 8</td><td></td><td></td><td>x</td><td></td></tr></table>	0 to 8 = F above 6 to 14 = D above 14 to 20 = C above 20 to 26 = B above 26 to 32 = A
Determine the points possible by multiplying the number of criteria by the number of point values.	$8 \times 4 = 32$	The example rubric earned 26 points, which falls in the B range.
Subtract the number of criteria from the points possible and divide by four to determine the remainder of point spans.	$(32 - 8)/4 = 6$	
Add the point span from step four to the high end of the "F" range to determine the "D" range. Repeat the process to determine each grade range.	$8 + 6 = 14$ $14 + 6 = 20$ $20 + 6 = 26$ $26 + 6 = 32$	

Figure 7.15: Changing a rubric score to a grade, solution 2.

In Conclusion

Rubrics are valuable tools for assessing students. The purpose of rubric use within the RTI framework is threefold:

1. A rubric provides students with the criteria important to the successful completion of a product, performance, or positive behavior.

2. The descriptors highlight the steps that lead to a quality outcome. The clear, up-front criteria and quality descriptors are intended to result in an increased number of students achieving success at Tier 1. Fewer students will need interventions, and those students needing extra support can be identified early through the use of data.

3. Rubric data can be used to compare students to their peers. Data can also be used to track individual progress. When progress is not appropriate, teachers can take steps to ensure future success.

Chapter 8

Performance Assessments for the 21st Century

Restricted-response test questions, such as true/false, short answer, multiple choice, and matching, measure students' "knowledge of performance, not the ability to actually carry out the performance" (Airasian, 2000, p. 145). Performance assessments, on the other hand, require students to carry out an activity or produce a product that demonstrates both knowledge and skill (Airasian, 2000).

Popham (2006) says that performance assessments are often called "performance tests" and although all educational tests require students to perform in some way, most educators think of performance tests as those that require students to construct an *original* response. Even though some educators believe that any form of constructed-response assessment could be classified as a performance assessment, others contend that genuine performance assessments must possess at least three features:

- *Multiple evaluative criteria.* The student's performance must be judged using more than one criterion. To illustrate, a student's ability to speak Spanish might be appraised on the basis of the student's accent, syntax, and vocabulary.

- *Prespecified quality standards.* Each of the criteria on which a student's performance is to be judged is clearly explicated in advance of evaluating the quality of the student's performance.

- *Judgmental appraisal.* Unlike the scoring of selected response tests in which electronic computers and scanning machines can, once programmed, carry on largely without the need of real people, performance assessments depend on human judgments to determine the acceptability of a student's performance. (Popham, 2006, pp. 233–234)

Some educators describe performance assessments as "authentic" assessments because the tasks closely mirror real-life, nonschool-related tasks that students will be expected to perform throughout their lives. These life skills will help prepare students for the rigors of work and to deal with their personal finances, health and well-being, social interactions, and citizenship.

With the increased emphasis on 21st century skills and reasoning strategies such as problem solving, analysis, investigation, and integration of technology, performance assessments have become the most accurate method for students to demonstrate that they are able to meet or exceed targeted curriculum outcomes and standards. Performance assessments also motivate students more than traditional pencil-and-paper assessments, and Marzano (2003) says there is a direct link between student motivation and achievement:

> If students are motivated to learn the content in any given subject, their achievement in that subject will most likely be good. If students are not motivated to learn the content, their achievement will likely be limited. (p. 144)

Struggling students may need additional help in meeting the challenges of the 21st century if they are going to be successful. Performance assessments allow students practice time to prepare for their final project or performance. During this formative process, teachers constantly check for understanding and provide feedback to all students, but some students may need targeted academic or behavioral interventions that go beyond the needs of the entire class. Teachers develop specific interventions to help get those students back on track before the final summative evaluation.

Such formative assessments could be considered the dress rehearsal, during which teachers direct and the students rehearse for the final evaluation on opening night. Some students are born actors and learn their lines and stage directions very quickly, whereas others may need extra rehearsals or even intensive coaching to prepare for their roles. The play is only as good as its entire cast, so the teacher/director provides responses to interventions as needed.

Performance Tasks

According to Popham (2006), there are two critical components of a performance test: "the *task* the student must attempt to carry out and the *rubric* (scoring guide) used to judge the adequacy with which the student has done that carrying out" (p. 235). A performance task is used to determine a student's ability to demonstrate skills. Based on the student's level of achievement, teachers can make an inference about the degree to which the student has mastered the targeted skill.

In today's diverse classroom, teachers must differentiate instruction to help struggling learners and to challenge students who master the concepts and tasks more quickly. Performance tasks often include group work, for which students can select projects or performances that interest them or be assigned to groups based upon their academic, social, or behavioral needs.

Performance tasks allow flexibility for student choice and provide time for teachers to work with individual students throughout the preparation period leading up to the final performance.

Performance tasks can take many forms, but they usually consist of a more formal goal such as a curricular aim or a targeted standard, a statement about what the students should know (declarative), and a statement about what the students should be able to do (procedural). They also usually focus on a problem scenario that the class must address using both group work to encourage collaboration and individual work to encourage student independence and accountability.

Performance tasks can be relatively simple and focus on one or more standards from a single discipline, or they can be complex and focus on multiple standards from multiple disciplines. A simple performance task could require students to write a letter to the editor about promoting better nutrition in the schools. A complex performance task could target multiple interdisciplinary content and process standards by requiring a student to conduct a schoolwide campaign to include more nutritional meals at the school, for example. The campaign could include research on food groups, an analysis of the cost of more nutritional foods, posters promoting better food choices by students, letters to the editor requesting local funding, letters and presentations to parents, meetings with school officials, conferences with the cafeteria manager, interviews with nutritionists, visitations to other school cafeterias, intercom commercials, and a schoolwide assembly. The complex performance task will obviously take more time, but it will address and connect multiple standards within a real-life context.

Authentic performance tasks require students to do more than just memorize facts. They require students to demonstrate their abilities to solve problems; utilize technology appropriately; formulate a problem; collect, analyze, and interpret data; make appropriate decisions; collaborate with others; and use both critical and creative thinking skills to address issues related to the workplace, national and international topics, and the challenges of the 21st century. These performance tasks could be in the form of oral presentations (debates, role-playing, mock trials, speeches, dramatic readings, Socratic questioning), written presentations (research papers, lab reports, word problems, historical analyses, résumés, literary critiques, plays, poetry, books, narratives, designs, informational writing, persuasive essays, responses to literature), or projects (science fairs, multimedia presentations, movies, models, dioramas, posters, pamphlets, maps, sculptures, artwork, simulation games, YouTube videos). Practices for oral presentations and rough drafts or sketches of projects would be considered formative assessments since students are in the learning stages and teachers are checking for understanding and providing feedback to improve student learning.

There are many templates that could be used to create performance tasks. Figure 8.1 (page 100) is an example of one form that presents a content- and grade-specific problem scenario to motivate students to write a persuasive essay about a current controversial topic related to the use of digital devices.

Subject Area: Language arts   **Unit**: Persuasive essay   **Grade Level**: 4–5

Standard: Students will write a persuasive essay that convinces the reader to think or act in a certain way about a controversial topic.

Declarative Knowledge (what students need to know): the components of a persuasive essay that convinces others to agree with the writer's opinions

Procedural Knowledge (what students need to do): use the writing process and the checklist provided to write a persuasive essay in the correct format

. . . .

Performance Task Scenario: *A recent study in a Kaiser Family Foundation survey of 2,002 people ages eight to eighteen shows that young people spend seven hours and thirty-eight minutes using media in a typical day. The study showed that media and mobile devices are now "part of the air" students breathe. Because of your mature abilities to manage digital devices and your vast expertise in writing, the third-grade teachers have asked you to research the impact of kids spending more than fifty-three hours a week using electronic media such as cell phones, iPods, video games, and computers. Once you have researched and analyzed the information, write the third graders* a persuasive essay *that either poses* and answers a question or *shows the* cause and effect *of digital decisions they make. Discuss how students' digital choices can affect their social interactions and academic careers. Let's get busy. We need those essays by April 20 because* the future of our third graders depends on you!

. . . .

Group Work: Research and analyze the data—Group 1: cell phones; Group 2: iPods; Group 3: video games; Group 4: computers.

Individual Work: Write a persuasive essay that either poses and answers a question or shows the cause and effect of the digital decisions students make.

Differentiations:

How can you adjust the degree of difficulty to provide more support? Allow students to use the persuasive essay checklist to help them organize and self-assess their work.

How can you adjust the task to challenge students to extend their thinking? Give the students the option to: (1) create a ten-slide PowerPoint presentation based on their research and arguments to present to the third graders; (2) Twitter the third-grade students with their thoughts; or (3) use a digital camera to capture student use of digital devices used during and after school.

Assessments: checklist and rubric for the persuasive essay

Figure 8.1: A Digital Disaster: A persuasive writing unit.

Figure 8.2 is an example of a performance task in a third-grade unit on elapsed time that will excite students about their upcoming field day. This assignment would add the motivating element of authenticity if the students were allowed to contribute to creating the real field-day schedule. When a task is relevant to the students' lives, they become more engaged in their own learning, and they see how important the concept is in real life. In this case, if they calculate incorrectly, they could end up missing one of their favorite activities or, worse, lunch!

Subject Area: Mathematics   **Unit**: Elapsed time   **Grade Level**: 3

Standard: Students will further develop their understanding of the concept of time by determining elapsed time of a full, half, and quarter hour.

Declarative Knowledge (what students need to know): the types of time segments and the concept of time

Procedural Knowledge (what students need to do): use their understanding of time to create appropriate schedules for events

. . . .

Performance Task Scenario: *Coach Weaver needs our help! He is so busy with the new puppy his wife brought home that he hasn't had time to schedule a field day for the third grade. Fortunately, he heard about our expertise in elapsed time and wants us to come up with the schedule for the third grade. These are some of the activities we can choose from: egg relay race, dizzy bat relay, tug-o-war, water balloon toss, Olympic torch relay, and up the ladder. To help him out, the third grade will create an elapsed-time schedule, an elapsed-time T-chart, a time line, and a map of activities showing time and location. We need to have this ready for Coach by April 28. Let's plan for the third-grade field day now!*

. . . .

Group Work: (1) Create an elapsed-time T-chart; (2) create a schedule of activities for the day; (3) write a time-order journal; and (4) create a map of activities listing times and locations.

Individual Work: Each student will complete either a time T-chart or a schedule for three to five activities for the field-day party.

Differentiations:

How can you adjust the degree of difficulty to provide more support? Provide a checklist for the group work to help students stay organized and on task.

How can you adjust the task to challenge students to extend their thinking? Ask students to create a trifold brochure of the field-day experiences using graphics.

Assessments: group-work checklist, individual-work rubric, standardized test, practice T-chart, practice schedule

Figure 8.2: Field-day Plans: Elapsed-time performance task for third grade.
Source: *Adapted from work created by James Kirk and Jennifer Vaught, teachers at Sharp Creek Elementary School, Carroll County Schools, Carrollton, Georgia. Used with permission.*

The field-day performance task should motivate the students to learn about elapsed time in order to plan their fun day. However, some students may not know where to begin when it comes to completing a T-chart for their field-day plans. Figure 8.3 (page 102) provides a group-work checklist to help students complete this task. Checklists also reduce classroom management problems because students know what they are expected to do and can follow a sequence of questions that guide them through the process.

Check your group work using the following criteria.	Not Yet 0	Yes 1
Did you make the T-chart?		
Did you identify six activities? What are they? 1. _____ 2. _____ 3. _____ 4. _____ 5. _____ 6. _____		
Did you identify the start time? _____		
Did you identify the end time? _____		
Did you identify the elapsed time? _____		
Did you organize your T-chart?		
Did you write a title on your T-chart? What is it? _____		
Is your T-chart neat so others can read it?		
Is your name on the back of your T-chart?		
Did your group work well together?		
Did you speak politely to others?		
Did you do your fair share of work? What did you do? Name _____ Job _____ Name _____ Job _____ Name _____ Job _____		
Did you listen to others' ideas?		

Total points: _____
Group comments: _____
Teacher comments: _____

Scale:

18–20 = Life of the party

16–17 = Just hanging out

14–15 = Went home early

Grade: _____

Figure 8.3: Field-day plans group-work T-chart checklist.

Source: *Created by James Kirk and Jennifer Vaught, teachers at Sharp Creek Elementary School, Carroll County Schools, Carrollton, Georgia. Used with permission.*

Group work is important because it allows students to practice their social skills and teachers to monitor student interactions. Individual work, however, is even more important because teachers are responsible for making sure each student can master the standards independently and consistently. Sometimes students within a group do not contribute or do not understand the concepts and rely on other group members to finish the task and cover for them. The group work serves as a rehearsal for the individual work. Usually the teacher models how to solve a problem, then the group members model how to solve a problem. Finally, it is time for each student to show what he or she can or cannot do.

The checklist in figure 8.4 provides scaffolding for all students, but it especially helps the struggling students with the individual-work task. Later in the learning process, the teacher can remove the scaffolding to make sure each student can complete the task without the extra support. Students in Tiers 2 or 3 may still require the checklist as well as additional interventions to master the task.

Check your individual work using the criteria below.	Not Yet 0	Yes 1
Ideas		
Did you create a list of at least three activities for the class to do (food, presentations, games)?		
Organization		
Did you identify the start time?		
Did you identify the end time?		
Did you identify the elapsed time?		
Did you write a title on your schedule? What is it?		
Is your schedule neat so others can read it?		
Is your name on the back of your schedule?		
Can we accomplish all of your activities in the allotted amount of time (do we get to go home on time)?		
Did you verify the correctness of your schedule?		
Conventions		
Did you spell your words correctly?		
Did you use colons when you wrote the time?		

Figure 8.4: Individual-work checklist for the field-day schedule.

Source: *Created by James Kirk and Jennifer Vaught, teachers at Sharp Creek Elementary School, Carroll County Schools, Carrollton, Georgia. Used with permission.*

Teachers can also provide students with a rubric that depicts in more detail the descriptors of quality work. The rubric in figure 8.5 asks the students to look at what they have included and see if they can improve the quality of their work, and their grade, by doing additional things. The rubric contains the same criteria as the checklist, but it is no longer written in question form.

In this example, the rubric is weighted to emphasize the math standard. The criteria listed in the organization section are weighted three times because this section covers the big idea of the math standard on elapsed time. The ideas and convention criteria are important for the task, but they are worth fewer points because they are not the focus of the lesson and the assessment.

Creating Performance Assessments

Most benchmark, short-cycle, interim, and standardized tests assess the lower levels of Bloom's taxonomy—recall and comprehension. Since performance assessments require students to analyze, synthesize, evaluate, and create products and performances, they target problem solving and higher-order thinking skills that are so crucial for success in the 21st century.

Teachers can draw upon real-world skills to create performance tasks that mirror the skills required for the workplace. For example, Linda Darling-Hammond (2010) of Stanford University states:

> At the high school level, performance tasks that assess career- and college-ready performance within and across disciplines should include research papers and presentations, literary analyses, science experiments, complex mathematical problem solutions and models, uses of technology, and exhibitions of learning from the arts, community service, and internships. (p. 300)

She recommends that these assessments be scored by teachers using common criteria (checklists and rubrics). This will ensure consistency in grading as well as provide students with constructive feedback connected to their career-related skills.

Some of the most motivating teacher-created and school-based performance tasks relate to current events, work-related events, or things happening in the classroom or the school. When students are given a choice regarding their topic or their method of presentation, they can select a task that interests them, and that choice provides a pathway to future success.

Fisher and Frey (2007) believe that performance-based learning is a critical component of differentiated learning because it allows students to showcase their competence in a variety of ways. They note:

> The importance of performance opportunities lies in their potential for providing other outlets for students to demonstrate their mastery of different concepts in ways that are not limited to more traditional school-based demonstrations such as reading, writing, and computational tasks. (p. 80)

Standard: Students will further develop their understanding of the concept of time by determining elapsed time of a full, half, and quarter hour.

Criteria	0 Stayed Home Sick	1 Went Home Early	2 Just Hanging Out	3 Life of the Party	Score
Ideas List of activities for the day: Egg relay race Dizzy bat relay Tug-o-war Water balloon toss Olympic torch relay Up the ladder	Zero activities on the list	One to two activities on the list	Three activities on the list	Four or more activities on the list	x 1 (3 points possible)
Organization Start time End time Elapsed time Title Neatness Name Accuracy	Zero to one items completed correctly	Two to five items completed correctly	Six items completed correctly	Seven items completed correctly	x 3 (9 points possible)
Conventions Spelling Punctuation	Spelling and punctuation errors make it difficult to understand	Some spelling and punctuation errors	Spelling or punctuation errors	Spelling and punctuation correct	x 1 (3 points possible)

Total Points: _____/15

Grade Equivalents:

A = 14–15 (93%–100%)

B = 12–13 (80%–87%)

C = 11 (73%)

Not yet = 0–10

Figure 8.5: Individual rubric for field-day schedule.

Source: *Created by James Kirk and Jennifer Vaught, teachers at Sharp Creek Elementary School, Carroll County Schools, Carrollton, Georgia. Used with permission.*

The results of these performance assessments will provide additional information about students' abilities for college success and potential employability that goes beyond the results of standardized test-score results.

Evelyn S. Johnson, Lori Smith, and Monica L. Harris (2009), authors of *How RTI Works in Secondary Schools*, discuss the importance of engaging middle school and high school students at the Tier 1 level, but especially at the Tier 2 level. If students reach middle school or high school without finding success at elementary school, they may become apathetic because they don't believe school will help them fulfill their future aspirations and goals. Johnson et al. (2009) say:

> Developing programs that address student motivation and self-esteem as well as exploration of career interests and life goals is very important. Therefore, tier 2 programming should include interventions that address motivational and goal-setting strategies as well as approaches for how to build learning communities. (p. 95)

When students work in teams to address a task that is meaningful and useful to them, they tend to get more involved with their learning because they feel more successful. They are able to see the value of their work in school and the workplace.

Teachers also need to work in teams, to design the performance task units. Popham (2006) warns that designing a performance assessment task and the rubric to accompany it takes a great deal of time. Teachers can make this task easier by collaborating. Some teacher teams even use electronic templates so it is easier to share their units.

Performance Task Scenarios

The most motivating part of the performance task is the scenario, which serves to hook the students. Once students can see an authentic purpose for the assignment, they are more likely to want to participate and complete the assignment. Following are some examples of scenarios.

Subject: Mathematics   **Unit**: Measurement   **Grade Level**: 2

Standard: Students will know the standard units of inch, foot, and yard and the metric units of centimeter and meter, and measure length to the nearest inch or centimeter.

Title: Bigfoot Has Been Sighted! How Big Is His Foot?

. . . .

Performance Task Scenario: Attention all students! We have a math emergency! *Bigfoot has been sighted in the woods behind our school.* MythBusters *has chosen our class to help determine if the creature Bigfoot really has a big foot! We need to identify and determine the appropriate tools for measuring Bigfoot's footprint. We will also need to estimate and measure the footprint found, compare it to our own footprints, and create a graph to show our findings. Let's get started, because the footprints are heading this way! YIKES!*

Source: *Created by Lisa Weaver, Keya Yarbrough, Sandra Prince, Tara Ferguson, and Donna Barnett, teachers at Sharp Creek Elementary School, Carroll County Schools, Carrollton, Georgia. Used with permission.*

Subject: Mathematics   **Unit**: Area of geometric plane figures   **Grade Level**: 5

Standard: Students will extend their understanding of the area of geometric plane figures.

Title: Royal Designs!

. . . .

Performance Task Scenario: *Attention, geometry gurus! As you know, Prince William and Kate were married in London. Living with the royal family and being hounded by the paparazzi has been very challenging for them, so they decided to build a new castle in the country. Because of your vast knowledge in geometric plane figures and your international reputations as junior architects, the couple would like you to design a modern and unique castle for them. They would like five of the rooms to be designed in the shapes of geometric plane figures. We need to divide into groups and create a design in the following shapes: irregular figure (Group 1), circle (Group 2), triangle (Group 3), parallelogram (Group 4), and rectangle (Group 5). They would like each group to create a poster of your room and find the area of your new design. Prince William and his bride want to see your blueprints in two weeks, so get your pencils ready and start sketching! We need to "shape up" for the royal family!*

Source: *Created by Jennifer Kanzler and Christina Gilbert, members of the PAGE Teacher Academy sponsored by the Professional Association of Georgia Educators on February 5, 2011, facilitated by Dr. Ann Stucke. Used with permission.*

Subject: Science   **Unit**: Living organisms   **Grade Level**: 7

Standard: Students will examine the evolution of living organisms through inherited characteristics that promote the survival of the organisms and the survival of successive generations of their offspring.

Element: Explain that physical characteristics of organisms have changed over successive generations (for example, Darwin's finches and peppered moths of Manchester).

Title: Infestation!

. . . .

Performance Task Scenario: *This is a public service announcement brought to you by the housing authority: You are being contacted by your local housing authority due to an infestation of bugs in your community. We need your help to figure out why current pesticides are not effective in removing the bugs. Currently there are four pests that are the most problematic, and each group will be assigned one of them: Group 1, bedbugs; Group 2, ladybugs; Group 3, termites; and Group 4, cockroaches. Each group will research how its pest has evolved and is now resistant to pesticides. Be prepared to share your findings with your community by completing the following activities:*

- *Activity 1: Create a pamphlet and a public service announcement.*

- *Activity 2: Design a detailed website (Facebook, MySpace, or wiki page).*

- *Activity 3: Present a detailed newscast to be broadcast in the neighborhood.*

- *Activity 4: Conduct a formal taped interview with appropriately researched questions with a pest control expert.*

Your research must be completed by Friday in order to present this vital information to members of your community before houses in a neighborhood near you will be condemned!

Source: *Created by Carla Hamilton, Jamie Strickland, Jessica Ruark, and Shiona Drummer, members of the PAGE Teacher Academy sponsored by the Professional Association of Georgia Educators on February 5, 2011, facilitated by Dr. Ann Stucke. Used with permission.*

Subject: Language arts   **Unit**: Essay writing   **Grade Level**: 9–12

Standard: Students will develop an effective essay using the narrative, informational, persuasive, or technical writing format.

Title: Free Wendell!

Performance Task Scenario: *Your buddy Wendell is in in-house suspension again! He really needs your help because Mr. Matthews, the dean of discipline, told Wendell that this is his last chance. He warned him that if he doesn't read the entire time he is in in-house suspension or if he falls asleep just once, he will be kicked out of school and sent off to boot camp in Alaska! Wendell can't stand to read and hates really cold places (he'd have to live in an igloo if he goes to that boot camp). Luckily, you and your partner can help. You must write a fascinating essay that Wendell can read while he is in his special room that will not bore him or put him to sleep. If it is dull and lacks structure, organization, or coherence, Wendell will be doomed, and it will be your fault! Your friend Wendell's fate is in your hands. He is counting on your essay to help him stay awake and avoid that frigid boot camp! Remember, if Wendell dozes off while reading your essay, he's toast!*

Source: *Created by Jacquelyn Brownlee, member of the PAGE Teacher Academy sponsored by the Professional Association of Georgia Educators on February 5, 2011, facilitated by Dr. Ann Stucke. Used with permission.*

Subject: British literature   **Unit**: Literary analysis and writing   **Grade Level**: 11–12

Standard: The student identifies, analyzes, and applies knowledge of the structures and elements of British literature and provides evidence from the text to support understanding.

Title: The Tale of the Missing Tale

Performance Task Scenario: *The original transcript of Geoffrey Chaucer's* The Canterbury Tales *was being delivered to the literature-loving queen of England. As the page was on his way to her castle, he stopped at the local mead hall for a short libation. Upon arriving at the queen's castle, he realized that one section of the manuscript had been blurred due to a spill and one of the famous tales was now illegible. In an effort to keep his head, he ran to the nearby Ye Old Schoolhouse to plead for help. You are a student in that schoolhouse, and it is your task to create a new tale that mimics Chaucer's original work so the queen is not suspicious. You have a few hours to create a new tale and help the tipsy page preserve his life. Your knowledge of Geoffrey Chaucer's style and the Canterbury tales is now a matter of life and death! Tap into your poetic creativity and spin a tale!*

Source: *Created by Cody Flowers, Lindsey Sherrouse, and Jacquelyn Brownlee, members of the PAGE Teacher Academy sponsored by the Professional Association of Georgia Educators on February 5, 2011, facilitated by Dr. Ann Stucke. Used with permission.*

21st Century Skills

According to Darling-Hammond (2010), the European and Asian nations that have improved student learning created curricula and assessments that outline core knowledge to focus on higher-order skills. She states that these are

> the abilities to find and organize information to solve problems, frame and conduct investigations, analyze and synthesize data, apply learning to new situations, self-monitor and improve one's own learning and performance, communicate well in multiple forms, work in teams, and learn independently. (p. 286)

One of the reasons performance tasks are being touted in education is because they require students to use both critical and creative problem-solving skills. Educators are beginning to focus on inquiry-oriented learning, emphasizing school-based formative assessments that require students to solve real problems and research and analyze relevant issues. These types of skills are difficult to assess using only restricted-response assessments such as multiple-choice questions. Therefore, it is essential that educators begin creating standards-based assessments designed to measure the thinking skills needed to complete the problem-based performance tasks.

Darling-Hammond (2010) says that Hong Kong is shaping its curricula and instruction around "critical thinking, problem solving, self-management skills, and collaboration. A particular concern is to develop meta-cognitive thinking skills, so students may identify their strengths and the areas that need additional work" (p. 291). Assessment systems that prioritize the usefulness and quality of information should also include school-created assessments that help teachers improve their teaching in order to improve student learning. Curriculum expert Heidi Hayes Jacobs (2010) encourages teachers to gradually phase out traditional assessments and begin to develop a pool of assessment replacements that are similar to the types of products and performances contemporary professionals might use in their jobs. She suggests that these professionals might produce documentaries, podcasts, digital music compositions, webcasts, online journals, online courses, blogs, video conferences, and films. She says that teachers will not be able to replace all their traditional assessments immediately, but they should stretch themselves by exploring resources such as interactive whiteboards, webcams, iPods, Photoshop, web quests, Wordle, and Moodle. Performance tasks should allow students to demonstrate what they can do with 21st century technological tools, which are often more familiar to them than to their teachers. By using these tools in the classroom today, they will be better prepared to meet the challenges of the workplace tomorrow.

Results from high-achieving countries indicate that the curriculum should be streamlined to reduce the emphasis on a laundry list of facts or activities that target lower-level thinking skills focused on memorization. By streamlining the curriculum, teachers can devote more time to helping students achieve deeper understanding of fewer meaningful concepts that can be transferred to everyday life. Of the curriculum, Darling-Hammond (2010) says:

It should allow students to study central ideas in a content area in ways that incorporate the important modes of inquiry in that domain—scientific investigation, mathematical reasoning, social scientific inquiry, literary analysis—enabling knowledge not just to be recalled but to be applied in ways that analyze, integrate, and use understandings in transferable ways. (p. 297)

In addition to focusing on meaningful curriculum goals, teachers have to engage their students. When students are intellectually engaged, learning takes place. Education consultant Charlotte Danielson (2009) says that in a high-energy classroom, students take pride in their work and work with their teachers as a joint enterprise to improve their classroom and their learning experiences. She says:

In a classroom in which everyone is deeply engaged, the teacher has managed to create a community of learners, in which everyone, especially the students, has "bought into" the work at hand. Students make active contributions to the idea being presented, and they may even have suggestions for how a certain part of a lesson should progress. (p. 55)

An inherent challenge at the secondary level is helping students overcome apathy and lack of motivation, which may have manifested in the elementary years but often become more intense throughout middle and high school. According to Johnson, Smith, and Harris (2009),

A lack of engagement can compound academic problems, and both aspects should be considered when designing a Tier 2 program. Tier 2 intervention must be designed to address the needs of and provide support to the fifteen to twenty percent of students who are failing to meet the demands and challenges of secondary school and consider dropping out as their only alternative. (p. 85)

Teachers should be provided with meaningful professional development opportunities that help them learn how to use the newly adopted research-based interventions aligned to the goals stated in the school improvement plan. Shores (2009) says that research has found a direct correlation between the learning curve of the students and the learning curve of the faculty and staff. She notes:

In high achieving schools, the adults are constantly seeking to improve their knowledge and skills for working with students. The staff development requirements for both academic and behavioral components of RTI implementation vary from school to school, but they are often quite extensive. (pp. 45–46)

Teachers who prefer to follow their textbooks and use the worksheets, quizzes, and tests provided by the publishers may be reluctant to create original assessments correlated to their state or provincial standards, in which case, it would be important to design professional development opportunities that increase their knowledge base and provide hands-on applications so these teachers can feel more confident creating original assessments. In addition to the training of classroom teachers, teachers and specialists who provide Tier 2 interventions should also be trained to deliver strategy-based instruction (Johnson et al., 2009).

Educators should try to shift students from their concern about only making good grades to their desire to become excited about learning. The traditional emphasis on stand-alone pieces of information needs to be updated to include a more integrated and higher-level approach to learning and using information in a meaningful and authentic context. Author Tim Tyson (2010) asks a question all educators should consider: "How do we move from an emphasis on remembering facts for a test on Friday to thinking critically about the larger issues that those disconnected facts can only dimly reflect as stand-alone pieces of information?" (p. 119).

Performance tasks require students to go beyond rote memorization of the facts and showcase their ability to use higher-order thinking skills. The most important skills students can attain and transfer to life involve the ability to think critically and creatively, solve problems, analyze data, and make decisions. Thinking should be the ultimate standard and the most important assessment.

Thinking Skills

Employers often perceive the new graduates entering the workforce as being deficient in the areas of critical thinking and problem solving (Casner-Lotto & Barrington, 2006, as cited in Pickering, 2010). Despite the thinking skills movement in the 1980s and 1990s, education consultant Debra Pickering (2010) asks, "Why do we not see evidence of improved thinking skills?" She says the reasons are multiple and complex, and we need to learn from our past mistakes. Setting high expectations for student thinking is not enough:

> Simply asking higher-order questions and then expecting higher-order answers is naïve. Cuing students to think hard—really, really hard—and expecting new insights and discoveries is fruitless. Scolding students for their lack of thinking and expecting these reprimands to motivate them to reach new levels is unfair. (Pickering, 2010, p. 147)

Teachers need to teach the thinking skills they expect.

Darling-Hammond (2010) believes that the efforts to create a "thinking curriculum" for all students are

> critically important to individual futures and our national welfare. Such efforts are unlikely to pay off, however, unless other central changes are made in the ways tests are used and accountability systems are designed, so that new standards and assessments inform more skillful and adaptive teaching that enables more successful learning for all students. (p. 300)

In all of the international standards, there is an emphasis on problem solving, decision making, conceptualizing, and other higher-order thinking skills and subskills. Rarely, however, do classroom assessments in North America today target thinking skills. Many curriculum units begin with an emphasis on the big ideas, enduring understandings, and essential questions that frame the units. Essential questions are posted on classroom blackboards; big ideas are posted on school bulletin boards; and teams of teachers spend a great deal of time working on the units to front-load all these thoughtful and reflective ideas. Many students, however, only value what is assessed. If teachers neglect to include mastery of these rigorous and relevant higher-level skills on their assessments, students focus on the lower-level factual questions that appear on their teacher-made or state or provincial tests because they know their grades will be based on their scores from those tests. Students who learn how to make decisions, generalize, brainstorm, prioritize, predict, and draw conclusions will be able to transfer those skills to all content areas. Facts become obsolete. The constant in all education involves students' ability to take control of their cognitive abilities and practice and improve them throughout their schooling and life.

Just like some students need a checklist to provide scaffolding to complete a task, some students need a checklist to help make an abstract thinking skill more concrete. They also need to know how to sequence the steps to arrive at the "aha" moment and to identify the specific thinking skill they are using. Being aware of the skill and being able to draw upon it when needed help them go beyond cognition into the realm of metacognition, where they "think about their thinking" and evaluate their effectiveness. Figure 8.6 shows a list of some important thinking strategies identified by Barry K. Beyer (1987), author of *Practical Strategies for the Teaching of Thinking*, as the most important "big ideas" of thinking.

Problem Solving

1. Recognize a problem.
2. Represent the problem.
3. Devise/choose a solution plan.
4. Execute the plan.
5. Evaluate the solution.

Decision Making

1. Define the goal.
2. Identify alternatives.
3. Analyze alternatives.
4. Rank alternatives.
5. Judge the highest-ranked alternatives.
6. Choose the "best" alternative.

Conceptualizing

1. Identify examples.

2. Identify common attributes.

3. Classify attributes.

4. Interrelate categories of attributes.

5. Identify additional examples/nonexamples.

6. Modify concept attributes/structure.

Figure 8.6: Thinking strategies.

Source: *Beyer, 1987, p. 44.*

Figure 8.7 lists thinking skills that have been classified according to *critical* thinking skills and *creative* thinking skills, but these two categories often overlap.

Critical Thinking Skills	Creative Thinking Skills
Attributing	Brainstorming
Determining cause and effect	Generalizing
Analyzing (comparing, contrasting, classifying)	Hypothesizing
Drawing a conclusion	Inventing
Evaluating	Making analogies
Prioritizing	Creating paradoxes
Sequencing	Personifying
Reasoning (inductive, deductive)	Predicting
Interpreting	

Figure 8.7: Critical and creative thinking skills.

If these skills or strategies have practical applications in students' lives (endurance), can be used in a number of subject areas (leverage), and are needed for the next level of instruction, they should be taught and assessed *explicitly* in the classroom. Teachers should evaluate these thinking skills with checklists and rubrics that help students self-assess their ability to apply targeted thinking skills in their performances. Figure 8.8 (page 114) shows an example of an elementary-level checklist for collecting, analyzing, and organizing information for a research report that was part of a performance task. By asking students to use the questions to guide their self-assessment, the teacher helps the students take control of their own learning. Students are accountable for writing in the answers rather than just checking off the "yes" box without really showing proof, allowing teachers to see where the students need help.

Standard: Students will collect, analyze, and organize information for a research report.		
Use this self-assessment checklist to guide you while you prepare a research report.	**Not Yet 0**	**Yes 1**
Data collection: Did you . . .		
Use an encyclopedia? Which one? _____		
Use a reliable Internet site? Which one? _____		
Use two other resources? List resources: _____		
Data analysis: Did you . . .		
Find three facts about your topic? List three facts: _____ _____ _____		
Restate your facts in your own words?		
Summarize your facts in one or two sentences:		
Organization of data: Did you . . .		
Develop an outline for your paper? List three main Roman numerals in your outline: I. _____ II. _____ III. _____		
Include a list of references? List three: _____ _____ _____		

Figure 8.8: Checklist for collecting, analyzing, and organizing information.

Another thinking skill that students need to master in order to analyze literature, science experiments, social studies events, or economics is that of determining cause and effect. Figure 8.9 (pages 115–116) takes elementary students through analyzing the cause-and-effect relationship of events in a story that was assigned as part of a performance task unit on literature.

Standard: Students will understand how to analyze cause-and-effect relationships.		
Self-assess your ability to read a story and analyze the cause-and-effect relationship of events.	**Not Yet** **0**	**Yes** **1**
Context of the situation: Can you . . .		
Identify and define the terms? List and define three terms: 1. _____ 2. _____ 3. _____		
See the direct relationships? Describe one:		
See the connections? Describe one:		
Chain of events: Can you . . .		
List the chain of events? 1. _____ 2. _____ 3. _____		
Prioritize the events? 1. _____ 2. _____ 3. _____		
Determine the differences between causes and effects?		
Causes: Can you list three causes?		
1.		
2.		
3.		

Continued on next page →

Effects: Can you list three effects?		
1.		
2.		
3.		
Analysis: Can you . . .		
Analyze the short-term effects? What are they?		
Analyze the long-term effects? What are they?		
Evaluate the relationships between the causes and the effects?		

Figure 8.9: Cause-and-effect checklist.

Some skills transfer into different content areas, but others focus on a specific subject area. Figure 8.10 shows a specific investigation checklist that takes middle school students step by step through conducting a scientific investigation that is embedded in a performance task unit to showcase their scientific inquiry skills. This formative assessment can later be developed into a rubric and eventually be used as a summative evaluation to determine a final grade.

Standard: Students will be able to conduct a scientific investigation.		
Criteria/Performance Indicators	**Not Yet** **0**	**Yes** **1**
Develop scientific inquiry skills: Did you . . .		
Conduct observations?		
Expand your knowledge base? How?		
Identify questions? List three: 1. _____ 2. _____ 3. _____		
Form a hypothesis? What is it?		
Design a scientific investigation? Describe it:		
Conduct a scientific investigation? Describe it:		

Appropriate tools and techniques: Did you . . .		
Gather data? What kind of data? List and describe the data:		
Analyze the data? How did you analyze the data? Explain:		
Interpret the data? What did you find out?		
Evidence: Did you use evidence to develop . . .		
Descriptions? Give an example:		
Explanations? Give an example:		
Predictions? Write two: 1. _____ 2. _____		
Models? Describe one:		
Critical and logical thinking skills: Did you . . .		
Make the relationship between evidence and explanations? Describe:		
Recognize alternative explanations and predictions? Explain:		
Analyze alternative explanations and predictions? Explain:		
Integrate mathematics into all aspects of inquiry? Give one example:		
Communication: Did you . . .		
Describe scientific procedures?		
Provide appropriate explanations?		
Evaluate the effectiveness of your inquiry? Explain how:		

Figure 8.10: Scientific investigation checklist.

Since problem solving is one of the major thinking strategies targeted in all performance tasks, it is important to help students self-assess their own problem-solving skills. Students should be able to demonstrate their ability to use a problem-solving process in all content areas, out-of-school activities, and the world of work. Figure 8.11 offers a series of questions to scaffold the steps to solve a problem that can be used for students in grades 4 through 12.

Standard: Students will develop a process to solve problems.		
Self-assess your problem-solving ability using this checklist.	**Not Yet 0**	**Yes 1**
Identification of problem: Did you . . .		
Identify important information? What is that information?		
Analyze data to find the real problem? What data? What is the real problem?		
Clarify the problem in your own words? Write a sentence:		
Prior knowledge: Did you . . .		
Think about similar problems? Name one:		
Identify the knowledge you will need? List it:		
Identify the skills you will need? Name them:		
Brainstorming possible solutions: Did you . . .		
Select the best solution? What is it?		
Adjust the solution as needed? How?		
Propose alternative strategies? Give one:		
Evaluation of solution: Did you . . .		
Collect data to document the effectiveness of the solution? What data?		
Solve the problem? Describe how:		
Understand the relationship between the problem and the solution? Explain:		

Transfer of problem-solving process: Can you . . .		
Solve similar problems in the future? Predict a similar problem:		
Solve problems independently and consistently? Self-assess your problem-solving ability:		
Predict potential sources of problems? Explain:		

Figure 8.11: Problem-solving checklist.
Source: *Burke, 2010, pp. 91–92.*

If teachers create performance tasks that require students to think outside the box and demonstrate higher-order thinking skills, it is counterproductive to provide assessments that only measure recall of factual information. If teachers expect students to think, they need to provide the same type of scaffolding for developing the thinking skill that they provide for the actual performance task project. Many students have difficulty making their abstract thinking concrete. All students need a framework to organize their thinking, but students in Tier 2 and Tier 3 may need more intensive scaffolding so they don't get frustrated and give up before they master the task and achieve success.

Richard Zagranski, William T. Whigham, and Patrice L. Dardenne (2008), authors of *Understanding Standards-Based Education*, describe the Statue of Liberty in New York Harbor when it was encased in scaffolding while being repaired for the bicentennial celebration. Once the renovation was completed successfully, the scaffolding was removed to reveal the finished product. The authors point out that "the support structure stands only as long as it is needed; it does not become a part of the finished product" (p. 108). The same is true in education. Scaffolding, such as checklists and rubrics for performance tasks, provide the proper support structure to eliminate problems or blocks that may confuse and frustrate all students, but especially confuse and frustrate struggling students. Gradually the teacher reduces the support structure because the students have developed new cognitive processes that assist them in making connections with what they already know and what they are learning. Zagranski et al. (2008) sum up the purpose of scaffolding nicely: "The goal of scaffolding is to allow students to do as much as they can on their own and then to provide the necessary steps, tools, models, or practices for the students to become self-regulated independent learners" (p. 109).

In Conclusion

Performance tasks are just one piece of the assessment process. They allow students to apply what they have learned in completing authentic tasks that simulate the types of problems, projects, and performances they will encounter in life. Feedback is provided throughout the tasks when teachers check for understanding.

Teachers use these formative assessments to adjust their teaching and develop effective interventions to help the students who have problems meeting the standards. Performance tasks that provide a real-life context will help teachers not only meet the diverse learning styles and behavior patterns of their students, but also address those ever-more important 21st century skills that are vital for student success.

The RTI framework provides a systematic approach to instruction and intervention in an effort to meet the needs of all students. A strong foundation at Tier 1 and beyond is built through the expertise and talents of teachers who are artists in the classroom and base their artistry on the implementation of research-based practices that will get results. Their well-rounded approach to classroom assessment equips them with information that can be used to determine what each student needs and to accurately respond to those needs in a timely and effective fashion.

The process of formative assessment promotes a cycle of continuous improvement that integrates instruction with assessment in a seamless loop in which teachers adapt immediately to students' needs. Students' knowledge and skills are evaluated using a variety of assessment tools ranging from checklists and rubrics to metacognitive reflections and authentic performance tasks. Data are collected and analyzed to determine the needs of both individuals and groups, and classroom instruction is tailored to respond to the needs identified as a result of assessment.

The impact of formative assessment within the RTI framework stems from its ability to quickly and effectively identify students' strengths and challenges. Assessment variety provides multiple opportunities and formats for students to show what they know. Analysis of performance and progress requires a response that will address student needs and increase the likelihood of successful outcomes.

RTI provides a systematic structure of learning and support. Formative assessment supplies the insight into student expertise. In union, the two create an approach that clearly aims to identify and meet the needs of all students.

References and Resources

Ainsworth, L., & Viegut, D. (2006). *Common formative assessments: How to connect standards-based instruction and assessment.* Thousand Oaks, CA: Corwin Press.

Airasian, P. W. (2000). *Assessment in the classroom: A concise approach* (2nd ed.). Boston: McGraw-Hill.

Appelbaum, M. (2009). *The one-stop guide to implementing RTI: Academic and behavioral interventions, K–12.* Thousand Oaks, CA: Corwin Press/Appelbaum Training Institute.

Belgrad, S., Burke, K., & Fogarty, R. (2008). *The portfolio connection: Student work linked to standards* (3rd ed.). Thousand Oaks, CA: Corwin Press.

Bender, W. N. (2003). *Relational discipline strategies for in-your-face kids.* Boston: Allyn & Bacon.

Bender, W. N. (2009). *Beyond the RTI pyramid: Solutions for the first years of implementation.* Bloomington, IN: Solution Tree Press.

Bender, W. N., & Larkin, M. J. (2009). *Reading strategies for elementary students with learning difficulties: Strategies for RTI* (2nd ed.). Thousand Oaks, CA: Corwin Press.

Bender, W., & Shores, C. (2007). *Response to intervention: A practical guide for every teacher.* Thousand Oaks, CA: Corwin Press.

Beyer, B. K. (1987). *Practical strategies for the teaching of thinking.* Boston: Allyn & Bacon.

Blankstein, A. M. (2004). *Failure is not an option: Six principles that guide student achievement in high-performing schools.* Thousand Oaks, CA: Corwin Press.

Brookhart, S. M. (2008). *How to give effective feedback to your students.* Alexandria, VA: Association for Supervision and Curriculum Development.

Brookhart, S. M. (2010). *How to assess higher-order thinking skills in your classroom.* Alexandria, VA: Association for Supervision and Curriculum Development.

Brown-Chidsey, R., & Steege, M. (2005). *Response to intervention: Principles and strategies for effective practice.* New York: Guilford Press.

Buffum, A., Mattos, M., & Weber, C. (2009). *Pyramid response to intervention: RTI, professional learning communities, and how to respond when kids don't learn.* Bloomington, IN: Solution Tree Press.

Burke, K. (2008). *What to do with the kid who . . . Developing cooperation, self-discipline, and responsibility in the classroom* (3rd ed.). Thousand Oaks, CA: Corwin Press.

Burke, K. (2009). *How to assess authentic learning* (5th ed.). Thousand Oaks, CA: Corwin Press.

Burke, K. (2010). *Balanced assessment: From formative to summative.* Bloomington, IN: Solution Tree Press.

Burke, K. (2011). *From standards to rubrics in six steps: Tools for assessing student learning* (3rd ed.). Thousand Oaks, CA: Corwin Press.

Burmark, L. (2002). *Visual literacy: Learn to see, see to learn.* Alexandria, VA: Association for Supervision and Curriculum Development.

Christopherson, J. T. (1997). The growing need for visual literacy at the university. In R. E. Griffin, J. M. Hunter, C. B. Schiffman, & W. J. Gibbs (Eds.), *VisionQuest: Journeys towards visual literacy* (pp. 169–174). University Park, PA: International Visual Literacy Association.

Costa, A. L., & Kallick, B. (1992). Reassessing assessment. In A. L. Costa, J. A. Bellanca, & R. Fogarty (Eds.), *If minds matter: A foreword to the future, volume II* (pp. 275–280). Palatine, IL: IRI/SkyLight Publishing.

Danielson, C. (2009). *Talk about teaching! Leading professional conversations.* Thousand Oaks, CA: National Staff Development Council/Corwin Press.

Darling-Hammond, L. (2010). *The flat world and education: How America's commitment to equity will determine our future.* New York: Teachers College Press.

DuFour, R., DuFour, R., Eaker, R., & Karhanek, G. (2010). *Raising the bar and closing the gap: Whatever it takes.* Bloomington, IN: Solution Tree Press.

DuFour, R., & Eaker, R. (1998). *Professional learning communities at work: Best practices for enhancing student achievement.* Bloomington, IN: Solution Tree Press.

Dunn, J. L. (1994). Television watchers. *Instructor, 103*(8), 50–54.

Fisher, D., & Frey, N. (2007). *Checking for understanding: Formative assessment techniques for your classroom.* Alexandria, VA: Association for Supervision and Curriculum Development.

Fisher, D., & Frey, N. (2010). *Enhancing RTI: How to ensure success with effective classroom instruction and intervention.* Alexandria, VA: Association for Supervision and Curriculum Development.

Frey, N., Fisher, D., & Everlove, S. (2009). *Productive group work: How to engage students, build teamwork, and promote understanding.* Alexandria, VA: Association for Supervision and Curriculum Development.

Gallavan, N. P. (2009). *Developing performance-based assessments: Grades K–5.* Thousand Oaks, CA: Corwin Press.

Gardner, H. (1993). *Frames of mind: The theory of multiple intelligences* (10th anniversary ed.). New York: Basic Books.

Gawande, A. (2010). *The checklist manifesto: How to get things right.* New York: Metropolitan Books.

Griffiths, A., Parson, L. B., Burns, M. K., VanDerHeyden, A., & Tilly, W. D. (2007). *Response to intervention: Research for practice.* Alexandria, VA: National Association of State Directors of Special Education.

Guskey, T. R. (2007). Using assessments to improve teaching and learning. In D. Reeves (Ed.), *Ahead of the curve: The power of assessment to transform teaching and learning* (pp. 15–29). Bloomington, IN: Solution Tree Press.

Guskey, T. R. (Ed.). (2009). *The teacher as assessment leader.* Bloomington, IN: Solution Tree Press.

Hall, S. L. (2008). *Implementing response to intervention: A principal's guide.* Thousand Oaks, CA: Corwin Press.

Henley, M. (2004). *Creating successful inclusion programs: Guidelines for teachers and administrators*. Bloomington, IN: Solution Tree Press.

Hoover, J. J. (2009). *RTI assessment essentials for struggling learners*. Thousand Oaks, CA: Corwin Press.

Howell, R., Patton, S., & Deiotte, M. (2008). *Understanding response to intervention: A practical guide to systemic implementation*. Bloomington, IN: Solution Tree Press.

Huff, S. (2009). Build, promote, guide, provide, monitor: Action words for principals as instructional leaders in assessment. In T. R. Guskey (Ed.), *The principal as assessment leader* (pp. 31–51). Bloomington, IN: Solution Tree Press.

Jacobs, H. H. (2010). Upgrading the curriculum: 21st century assessment types and skills. In H. H. Jacobs (Ed.), *Curriculum 21: Essential education for a changing world* (pp. 18–29). Alexandria, VA: Association for Supervision and Curriculum Development.

Johnson, E. S., Smith, L., & Harris, M. L. (2009). *How RTI works in secondary schools*. Thousand Oaks, CA: Corwin Press.

Joyce, B., & Calhoun, E. (2010). *Models of professional development: A celebration of educators*. Thousand Oaks, CA: Corwin Press.

Lezotte, L. W. (1992). *Creating the total quality effective school*. Okemos, MI: Effective Schools Products.

Lindstrom, R. L. (1999, April 19). Being visual: The emerging visual enterprise. *Business Week*, Special Advertising section.

Lunsford, A. A., & Ruszkiewicz, J. J. (2009). *Everything's an argument*. New York: Bedford/St. Martin's.

Marzano, R. J. (2003). *What works in schools: Translating research into action*. Alexandria, VA: Association for Supervision and Curriculum Development.

Marzano, R. J. (2007). *The art and science of teaching: A comprehensive framework for effective instruction*. Alexandria, VA: Association for Supervision and Curriculum Development.

Marzano, R. J., Pickering, D. J., & Pollock, J. E. (2001). *Classroom instruction that works: Research-based strategies for increasing student achievement*. Alexandria, VA: Association for Supervision and Curriculum Development.

Mellard, D. F., & Johnson, E. (2008). *RTI: A practitioner's guide to implementing response to intervention*. Thousand Oaks, CA: Corwin Press.

Moss, C. M., & Brookhart, S. M. (2009). *Advancing formative assessment in every classroom: A guide for instructional leaders*. Alexandria, VA: Association for Supervision and Curriculum Development.

Nielsen Wire. (2010, October 14). U.S. teen mobile report: Calling yesterday, texting today, using apps tomorrow [Blog post]. Accessed at http://blog.nielsen.com/nielsenwire/online_mobile/u-s-teen-mobile-report-calling-yesterday-texting-today-using-apps-tomorrow on February 9, 2011.

O'Connor, K. (2009). *How to grade for learning: Linking grades to standards*. Thousand Oaks, CA: Corwin Press.

Ogle, D. (1986). K-W-L: A teaching model that develops active reading of expository text. *The Reading Teacher, 39*(6), 564–570.

Paivio, A. (1986). *Mental representations: A dual coding approach.* New York: Oxford University Press.

Phillips, V., & Wong, C. (2010). Tying together the common core of standards, instruction, and assessments. *Phi Delta Kappan, 91*(5), 37–42.

Pickering, D. (2010). Teaching the thinking skills that higher-order tasks demand. In R. J. Marzano (Ed.), *On excellence in teaching* (pp. 145–166). Bloomington, IN: Solution Tree Press.

Popham, W. J. (2002). *Classroom assessment: What teachers need to know* (4th ed.). Boston: Allyn & Bacon.

Popham, W. J. (2006). *Assessment for educational leaders.* Boston: Pearson/Allyn & Bacon.

Popham, W. J. (2008). *Transformative assessment.* Alexandria, VA: Association for Supervision and Curriculum Development.

Prensky, M. (2001). Digital natives, digital immigrants: A new way to look at ourselves and our kids. *On the Horizon, 9*(5). Accessed at www.marcprensky.com/writing/Prensky%20-%20Digital%20Natives,%20Digital%20Immigrants%20-%20Part1.pdf on March 22, 2011.

Rakes, G. C. (1999). Teaching visual literacy in a multimedia age. *TechTrends, 43*(4), 14–15.

Reeves, D. B. (2002). *The leader's guide to standards: A blueprint for educational equity and excellence.* San Francisco: Jossey-Bass.

Reeves, D. B. (2004). *Assessing educational leaders: Evaluating performance for improved individual and organizational results.* Thousand Oaks, CA: Corwin Press.

Reeves, D. B. (2010). *Transforming professional development into student results.* Alexandria, VA: Association for Supervision and Curriculum Development.

Reider, B. (2005). *Teach more and discipline less: Preventing problem behaviors in the K–6 classroom.* Thousand Oaks, CA: Corwin Press.

Rosen, L. D. (2011). Teaching the iGeneration. *Educational Leadership, 68*(5), 10–15.

Schmoker, M. (2006). *Results now: How we can achieve unprecedented improvements in teaching and learning.* Alexandria, VA: Association for Supervision and Curriculum Development.

Schmoker, M. (2011). *FOCUS: Elevating the essentials to radically improve student learning.* Alexandria, VA: Association for Supervision and Curriculum Development.

Senge, P. (2000). *Schools that learn: A fifth discipline fieldbook for educators, parents, and everyone who cares about education.* New York: Doubleday.

Shores, C. (2009). *A comprehensive RTI model: Integrating behavioral and academic interventions.* Thousand Oaks, CA: Corwin Press.

Shores, C., & Chester, K. (2009). *Using RTI for school improvement: Raising every student's achievement scores.* Thousand Oaks, CA: Corwin Press; Arlington, VA: Council for Exceptional Children.

Small, M. (2009). *Good questions: Great ways to differentiate mathematics instruction.* New York: Teachers College Press; Reston, VA: National Council of Teachers of Mathematics; Toronto, ON: Nelson Education.

Snyder, T. D. (2010). *Mini-digest of educational statistics, 2009.* Washington, DC: National Center for Education Statistics.

Stiggins, R. (2007). Assessment through student eyes. *Educational Leadership, 64*(8), 22–26.

Tyson, T. (2010). Making learning irresistible: Extending the journey of Mabry Middle School. In H. H. Jacobs (Ed.), *Curriculum 21: Essential education for a changing world* (pp. 115–132). Alexandria, VA: Association for Supervision and Curriculum Development.

Wiggins, G., & McTighe, J. (2007). *Schooling by design: Mission, action, and achievement.* Alexandria, VA: Association for Supervision and Curriculum Development.

Wolk, R. A. (2011). *Wasting minds: Why our education system is failing and what we can do about it.* Alexandria, VA: Association for Supervision and Curriculum Development.

Wright, J. (2007). *RTI toolkit: A practical guide for schools.* Port Chester, NY: Dude.

Zagranski, R., Whigham, W. T., & Dardenne, P. L. (2008). *Understanding standards-based education: A practical guide for teachers and administrators.* Thousand Oaks, CA: Corwin Press.

Index

Balanced Assessment: From Formative to Summative
Kay Burke

Learn how to integrate formative and summative assessments seamlessly into instruction. The research, rationale, strategies, and examples provided in this book will help teachers develop their own repertoire of formative and summative assessments to monitor, grade, and make inferences about a student's ability to meet standards and curriculum goals. Exercises at the end of each chapter provide opportunities to reflect and plan action steps.
BKF272

The Teacher as Assessment Leader
Edited by Thomas R. Guskey

Meaningful examples, expert research, and real-life experiences illustrate the capacity and responsibility every educator has to ignite positive change. Packed with practical strategies for designing, analyzing, and using assessments, this book shows how to turn best practices into usable solutions.
BKF345

Ahead of the Curve: The Power of Assessment to Transform Teaching and Learning
Edited by Douglas Reeves

Leaders in education contribute their perspectives of effective assessment design and implementation, sending out a call for redirecting assessment to improve student achievement and inform instruction.
BKF232

Formative Assessment & Standards-Based Grading
Robert J. Marzano

Learn everything you need to know to implement an integrated system of assessment and grading. Dr. Marzano explains how to design, interpret, and systematically use three different types of formative assessments and how to track student progress and assign meaningful grades.
BKL003

Beyond the RTI Pyramid: Solutions for the First Years of Implementation
William N. Bender

This book helps schools deepen the RTI experience by extending the processes beyond initial implementation. Examples from real schools show how to apply RTI in reading, math, and behavior at elementary and secondary schools. All critical stakeholders in the school community will get a clear sense of their contribution to successful implementation.
BKF280

Solution Tree | Press

a division of
Solution Tree

Visit solution-tree.com or call 800.733.6786 to order.